Bundy:
Portrait of a Serial Killer

Robert Keller

Please Leave Your Review of This Book At
http://bit.ly/kellerbooks

ISBN-13: 978-1548730673

ISBN-10: 154873067X

robertkellerauthor.com

Table of Contents

Introduction

It is a question I am asked often, one that seemingly occupies the mind of just about every true crime reader I meet. Usually it is phrased something like this. "What makes a serial killer? What compels them to kill?"

I have spent many years, decades even, puzzling over that same question. As far as I can tell it is a combination of genetics, environment and experiences, mashed together in countless different ways to produce its monstrous outcome. (I wrote an article on the subject which you can read here, if you're interested: What Makes a Serial Killer?).

But even these findings, intended to distill my thoughts into a definitive answer, left me unfulfilled. There had to be something more, something I was missing. Gradually, I came to realize what it was. Only a psychopath can truly understand the thoughts and motives of another psychopath. These days, when people ask me "What makes a serial killer?" I tell them to study Ted Bundy.

Theodore Robert Bundy was America's ultimate bogeyman, the quintessential sex slayer, a demon in the guise of an ordinary man. But this was no hunched gargoyle, wild-eyed and foaming at the mouth to warn us of his bad intentions. This was a handsome, talented and articulate young man, an honors graduate for whom a bright future was predicted. This was a rising star in the

Republican Party who might well have achieved his ambition of high political office. (President Bundy has a nice ring to it, don't you think?)

Except Ted Bundy chose a different path, a path that would lead him into the darkest reaches of the human soul, a place where angels genuinely would fear to tread. He would not make that journey alone, at least 36 young women would make it with him, albeit unwillingly.

What is fascinating about the Bundy story is that there is a clear descent. The road to hell in this case has well-defined markers. Bundy went from being a habitual thief to being a chronic masturbator obsessed with porn. He then started making clumsy attempts at disabling women's cars. From there it wasn't a huge leap to stalking Co-Eds through the darkened streets around the University of Washington campus, to peeking into windows, to admitting to himself that his enjoyment at seeing their naked flesh was more than sexual, that his arousal relied on the idea of causing them harm.

That realization frightened him, terrified him so much that he swore off his nocturnal rambles and stayed off the streets for a full three months. But all the while, the tension was building. Like any addiction, this wasn't one that could be overcome simply by wishing it away.

And so Bundy returned to wandering the alleyways and thoroughfares of his neighborhood, now numbing his senses with alcohol to ward off any prickling of conscience that he might encounter. Then came the night when he picked up a chunk of wood with the express intention of causing harm to the woman he was stalking. And then came the night when he followed through on that intent.

All of these steps happened by small degrees and if Bundy is to be believed, then the "normal Ted" fought the "entity" (as he dubbed his murderous alter-ego) every step of the way. I am not so sure. In fact, I reject categorically Bundy's assertion that he tried to keep the "entity" in check. Such attempts would have been futile, in any case. Bundy was on a path that had only one destination. Eventually, he was going to cause harm to some unfortunate woman. Serious harm. On January 5, 1974, Bundy entered a student's apartment and beat her senseless. Less than a month later, he spirited Lynda Ann Healy away into the night.

At first, murder was a matter of expedience, to eliminate the possibility of being caught, as Bundy put it. But Bundy quickly developed a taste for killing. He became obsessed with death. He invented ingenious ways of luring his victims and delighted in the thrill of the hunt. Possession was his aim, and what better way of possessing someone than by taking that person's life. But Bundy didn't stop there. He now entered a phase of accelerating depravity.

We know what Bundy did once he had a rapidly cooling corpse at his feet and we know what he did to the decomposing remains in the weeks that followed. We know because Bundy liked to talk. Many of those harrowing details were shared with authors Michaud and Aynesworth, with Dr. Robert Keppel, with FBI Special Agent William Hagmaier. Some are so extreme that the gentlemen in question refuse to divulge them, even to this day.

And so to the question I asked earlier, "What makes a serial killer?" and to the answer I suggested, "study Ted Bundy." That Bundy was a psychopath is undoubted. That he was possessed of extremely aberrant sexual drives is also true. And yet, if there is any deviant who might have found a way out of the maze, it is he. The tools were all there – an above average intellect, a solid education, powerful contacts, good looks, the love of a beautiful, cultured and wealthy woman. Even these could not assuage the murderous compulsion fermenting in Bundy's brain. They couldn't because Bundy didn't want them to.

In truth, Ted Bundy never stood a chance. His cravings were far too powerful, far too addictive. His was an alien brain, an insect brain. His thought patterns cannot be understood by comparison with those of a normal human being. Although the idea was once derided, many psychiatrists now believe that there are those among us who are born evil. Ted Bundy fits that mold. There is no possibility that he could have become anything other than the monster he became.

Chapter 1: Beginnings

Her name was Eleanor Louise Cowell, she was 22 years old and she was pregnant. Nothing unusual in that, of course, young women become pregnant every day and usually it is a joyous discovery. Except that Eleanor was unmarried and this was 1946, an era in which good girls simply did not get themselves "knocked-up." An unwed woman who found herself expectant back then, brought dishonor on herself and on her kin. And it was this latter issue that concerned Eleanor most. Her family was prominent in their Philadelphia community, deeply religious, her father a church elder. The news was not going to sit well with him.

All of this left Eleanor with a conundrum to solve. The way she saw it, she had three choices. One of those, the termination option, she dismissed right away. Abortions were illegal back then, performed in grimy backrooms by men and women of questionable medical expertise. Besides, abortion did not gel with Eleanor's religious beliefs so it was definitely off the table.

What then of adoption? That, of course, was the sensible choice. She could move out of state before her pregnancy became too obvious, have the child, and then give it up. No one would be any the wiser. But Eleanor knew, knew in her heart of hearts, that she wasn't going to be able to do that. She already felt a deep bond with the child growing within her. Whatever the circumstances of its conception, this was her flesh and blood. Let the gossips say

what they would. Let them call her a tramp and her child a
bastard. She was holding on to it.

And so, with that resolved, Eleanor Cowell presented her parents
with the news that she was sure would shatter their lives.
Eleanor's mother (also named Eleanor) was a diminutive woman
who, like her daughter, barely topped five-foot tall. She was of a
nervous disposition and had received shock therapy for
depression. This is perhaps unsurprising when you consider the
personality of her husband. Samuel Cowell was an overbearing
and cruel man who ruled his family with an iron fist. He was prone
to outbursts of temper during which he'd strike out at anyone in
his immediate vicinity. The family pets suffered horribly at his
hands, as did his wife and children. On one occasion, he threw his
daughter Julia down a flight of stairs as punishment for
oversleeping. He was also a bigot and a racist who held blacks,
Jews and Catholics in particular contempt. Notwithstanding his
position as a respected church elder, he was addicted to
pornography and kept a stash of girly magazines in a garden shed.
Eleanor had genuine cause to be afraid of his response when she
made her announcement.

But to Eleanor's surprise, her father handled the news fairly well.
In fact, after a few hours of reflection, he came up with a scheme
by which Eleanor could keep her child and also hold onto her
reputation.

And so it was that the seven-months pregnant Eleanor Cowell
departed Philadelphia in September 1946 and took up residence
at the Elizabeth Lund Home for Unwed Mothers in Burlington,

Vermont. There, on November 24, 1946, she gave birth to a healthy baby boy who she named Theodore Robert Cowell. She refused to reveal the identity of the child's father, saying only that he was a sailor.

A few weeks after the birth, Eleanor and her son moved back into her parents' home in Philadelphia. Now the second part of Samuel Cowell's plan swung into action. The baby, affectionately known as Ted, was presented to the world as the offspring of Samuel and his wife. He would grow up believing that his real mother was his sister.

Ted Bundy as a child

Ted grew to be a bright young boy, much loved by his grandparents/parents, by his mother/sister, and by the two aunts who he believed were his siblings. It was clear from an early age that he was a child of remarkable intelligence. But there were signs too that all was not right with the boy. At the age of just three, he was sneaking into the garden shed to browse his grandfather's porn collection. Then in March 1950, there was an incident which in retrospect seems like a frightening portent of what was to come. One morning, Ted's aunt Julia woke to find him standing at the foot of her bed, a peculiar smile on his face. The three-year-old had carried up all of the knives from the kitchen and had arranged them around his sleeping aunt, with the blades facing inward.

Whether that incident had anything to do with Eleanor's decision to leave her parental home is unknown. In truth, there were probably other factors that drove the decision. Samuel Cowell's cover story regarding Ted's parentage may have been believed by friends and acquaintances but the extended Cowell clan was less convinced. Eleanor was fearful that Ted would learn the truth from them as he grew older. She was also fed up with living under her father's despotic rule. And so, in October 1950, Eleanor announced that she and her son were moving out west, to Washington State.

Chapter 2: Growing up Bundy

The move must have been traumatic to Ted. How do you explain to a four-year-old that he is being taken away from his "mother and father" and sent away with his "sister?" Moreover, Ted had a close bond with Samuel Cowell. In later years, he'd recall his grandfather in glowing terms. (Some psychiatrists have speculated that this was a picture concocted as a coping mechanism. They believe that Ted may have lived in terror of his violent and overbearing "father.")

Whatever the case, young Ted was taken by his mother to Tacoma, Washington, where she had family. In keeping with the new start, Eleanor began using her middle name, Louise. And Ted had a new name too. Prior to leaving Philadelphia, his mother had changed his last name by deed poll to Nelson. (This perhaps was an effort to conceal the truth about his paternity).

Like most youngsters, the newly-named Ted Nelson adapted quickly to his new surroundings. He had cousins, Alan and Jane Scott, who were about his age and the three of them were soon inseparable. As for Louise, she found a secretarial job and became active in the local Methodist Church. It was at a church function that she met her future husband, John Culpepper Bundy.

Bundy was a cook who worked at the nearby Madigan Army Hospital. He was a shy young man who stood barely taller than

Louise at 5-foot-one. Eventually, he plucked up the courage to ask her out on a date and within just a few months the couple had announced their engagement. They married on May 19, 1951, with Bundy officially adopting Louise's five-year-old son. Ted Nelson was now Theodore Robert Bundy.

Ted Bundy may have acquired his stepfather's last name but he held a very low opinion of the man his mother had married. Johnny did his best to build up a rapport with his stepson but Ted generally held him at arm's length. When Johnny planned camping trips or other father-son type activities, he'd cry off, citing homework or saying that he felt unwell. Years later he'd describe Johnny as "not too bright."

Ted's relationship with the four children that Louise had by Johnny Bundy was only slightly better. Most of the time he preferred to be alone. He did, however, appear close to the youngest of his stepsiblings, born when Ted was 15 years old. Often he'd have to babysit the youngster and he seemed to enjoy their time together, even though it kept him from hanging out with kids his own age. Perhaps he preferred that because at the age of 15, Ted Bundy was exceedingly shy and uncomfortable in social situations. It caused him to develop a stutter when put on the spot and that, in turn, led to him being bullied in junior high. Notwithstanding that treatment, he managed to maintain a solid grade-point average, earning mainly A's and B's.

This was Ted Bundy at 15, a neat and exceptionally well-mannered young man who did well at school, had a newspaper route and spent the rest of his spare time babysitting his younger siblings.

But that tells only part of the story. Unbeknownst to his parents, Ted had developed some troubling behaviors. He liked to go wandering around the neighborhood, rummaging through trash cans for the pornographic magazines that he sometimes found discarded there. He had also become a prolific shoplifter, stealing for the thrill of it rather than for any material gain. And then, in 1961, there was another incident, a far more serious incident. An eight-year-old girl went missing from the neighborhood, along the newspaper route that Ted worked.

The disappearance of Ann Marie Burr has never been positively linked to Ted Bundy. In fact, the main suspect at the time was another youth, a 17-year-old who lived close to the Burr residence. He was questioned (including under polygraph) and subsequently released without charge. Ann Marie Burr has never been found.

So what is Ted Bundy's connection to the Burr case? It all comes down to a throwaway remark he made to investigator Bob Keppel in 1989. Bundy had by now confessed to a slew of murders but he told Keppel that there are some he would never admit to, "murder committed at a young age, against a child victim, and close to his own home." The Burr case matches all three of these criteria.

Whether or not Ann Marie Burr was Ted Bundy's first victim or not is open to conjecture. But we do know that by this time, his inner dialog had become ever more aberrant. His taste in pornography had begun to veer from the standard softcore photo arrays to specialist magazines depicting violence against women. His shoplifting activities had escalated. He had started wandering his neighborhood at night, peeking into windows. And he had begun fantasizing about committing acts of sexual violence.

High School Yearbook picture of Ted Bundy

On the surface though, the façade held firm. He continued to do well academically, graduating eventually from Woodrow Wilson High School with a 'B' average. That gained him admission to the University of Puget Sound for the academic year 1965-66 although he transferred the next summer to the University of Washington where he registered for a course in Chinese. His reason for choosing that particular major was remarkably intuitive. Ted believed that China was the rising world power and that fluency in the language was imperative for the future. Already, he had one eye on a career in politics.

Ted had by now grown into a tall, handsome six-footer, always impeccably turned out and with the kind of old-world good manners that could not help but impress a girl. And yet, at age 20, he'd never had a relationship with a woman. Part of that could be attributed to his shyness but another was to do with the exceedingly high standards he set. Ted Bundy had no doubt that he was destined for greater things and the woman he chose to share his life would have to reflect that. She had to be beautiful, refined, and from a moneyed background. In the Spring of 1967, he found her.

Chapter 3: Rise and Fall

Stephanie Brooks ticked all the right boxes. Ted thought that she was the most beautiful girl he'd ever seen and she was from a wealthy Californian family. Still he wavered, unsure of himself. Why would such a refined woman be interested in a middle-class bumpkin like him? His natural insecurity alerted, he watched her from a distance for some time before he built up the courage to approach. By then, he had uncovered one area of commonality between them. They both loved to ski. It would be that activity that opened his path into Stephanie's life. To his surprise, she was receptive to his advances and within a short time they were an item.

Stephanie was fond of Ted but probably not as much in love with him as he was with her. She was a serious young woman, as eager to get ahead in the world as he was. And she wasn't sure that Ted Bundy was the man she wanted by her side on her journey. He was immature for starters, overly emotional and somewhat shiftless. She also knew that he used people, that he lied easily and often borrowed money with no intention of ever paying it back. She had a suspicion that he sometimes cheated on her.

And so, when Stephanie graduated from UW in June 1968, she decided to call time on the relationship. She didn't explicitly tell Ted that it was over but she figured that with her leaving Seattle and moving to San Francisco to take up a job, the relationship would die a natural death. She was wrong. Ted applied for and won a summer scholarship to Stanford University to study Chinese. He found an apartment just a few miles from Stephanie's parents' home and they continued to date until the eve of Ted's return to Seattle. That was when Stephanie sat him down for a talk and told him it was over.

Ted was devastated by the breakup. Back at UW he abandoned his Chinese studies and switched to a course in urban planning and sociology. But that couldn't hold his attention either and he soon dropped out of college altogether.

As the year 1969 dawned, Ted Bundy was still floundering, still hurting over Stephanie's betrayal, still trying to come to terms with his new reality. It is perhaps for this reason that he decided to travel back East, to Philadelphia, to visit his family. While he was there, he registered for classes at Temple University but that had never been the purpose of his visit. What he really wanted was some closure as to his parentage.

Ted was no fool, and he'd long suspected that the cover story told by Louise was a lie. Bizarrely, Louise had kept up the charade, even after her marriage to Johnny Bundy. When it would have been easy enough for her to tell Ted the truth about his conception and birth, she chose to remain silent. It led to the odd situation where Ted sometimes called her "Louise" and sometimes, "Mom." Now he finally had his suspicions confirmed. In Burlington, Vermont, he learned that Louise was really his mother. His father, according to the documentation, was a man named Lloyd Marshall, a graduate of the University of Pennsylvania and an Airforce veteran who listed his occupation as "salesman." That knowledge should perhaps have brought some closure to Bundy. Instead it left him feeling more empty than ever.

There are two ways that Ted could have responded to the twin blows of losing Stephanie and finding out the truth about his parentage. He could have fallen apart, losing himself in a binge of booze and self-pity, or he could have resolved there and then to get his life together, to steer his ship back on course. It is to his credit that he not only chose the latter but was able to pull it off. In the fall semester of 1969, he was back on the University of Washington campus, enrolled in a new course of study. And in psychology, Ted appeared to have found his niche. He excelled, pulling down mostly A's and earning the praise and admiration of his professors. The young man who'd flunked out of a course in urban planning would go on to graduate with honors.

Things were looking up on the personal front too. On September 26, 1969, Ted was drinking in the Sandpiper Tavern when he met the woman who would have a greater impact on his life than any other, save perhaps for his mother. Elizabeth Kloepfer was a couple of years older than Ted, a divorcee with a young daughter. She did not fit the mold of Ted's ideal woman like Stephanie did, but she was petite and somewhat attractive and the daughter of a prominent doctor from Utah. She'd moved to Seattle after the breakdown of her marriage and knew nobody there, save for one friend from her home state.

Liz Kloepfer might not have matched Ted's idealized standard of womanhood but there was one thing she could give him that Stephanie could not, unconditional love. Virtually from the time of their first meeting, Liz was entirely besotted with Ted. She would maintain that devotion even when she suspected that he was cheating on her with other women, even when she suspected that he was a habitual thief and petty criminal, even when she suspected that his criminal activities were far, far worse than that.

For now, though, Ted must have seemed to Liz like a gift from heaven. He was loving, caring and attentive, not just to her but also to her four-year-old daughter, Tina. And his life seemed to be on a steep upward trajectory. He'd recently been appointed a precinct committeeman for the local Republican Party. And he was a decorated hero. In 1970, Ted received a commendation from the Seattle police department after he chased down and apprehended a bag snatcher. That same summer he waded into Seattle's Green Lake to save a toddler from drowning. He saved other lives too, as a volunteer at the Seattle Crisis Clinic, working the lines from 9 p.m. to 9 a.m. several nights a week. He also interned as a psychiatric counsellor at Harborview Medical Center.

But it was always politics that had intrigued Ted. He spoke (only half-jokingly) of becoming Governor of Washington someday. So when the opportunity arose to work on Governor Dan Evans' re-election drive, he jumped at it. After the successful conclusion of that campaign, he found himself working for Seattle's Crime Prevention Advisory Commission, reviewing amendments to Washington's new hitchhiking laws. By then, he'd already decided to pursue a degree in law and applied to the University of Utah, with a personal letter of recommendation from Governor Dan Evans.

Ted would ultimately be accepted into Utah Law but in the fall of 1973, weeks before the first semester was about to begin, he wrote to the Dean of Admissions saying that he regretfully would not be able to take up the offer. He cited an automobile accident, which he claimed had left him hospitalized and incapacitated. In truth, it had been a fender bender and he'd suffered no more than a sprained ankle.

No one knows why Bundy chose not to attend Utah Law when he'd worked so hard to get into the school in the first place. However, his acceptance into the college would play an important part later in the story.

For now, Bundy picked up his law studies at the University of Puget Sound, attending classes on Mondays, Wednesdays, and Fridays. And he soon had a new job in politics, as assistant to Ross Davis, chairman of the Republican Party in Washington State.

One might wonder at this dramatic transformation in Ted Bundy, from college dropout to honors student, from rootless, immature young man to rising political star. What drove him to make such a dramatic shift? The answer to that question existed only in Ted Bundy's mind. One woman, however, was about to find out. To her cost.

By 1973, Ted and Stephanie Brooks had been apart for four years. During that time, Ted had been in an apparently committed relationship with Elizabeth Kloepfer. But he'd never given up on winning back Stephanie's heart and in the summer of '73 he felt he was ready to make his play. While on Republican Party business in Sacramento, he contacted Stephanie in San Francisco and arranged to meet her.

Just as Ted had intended, Stephanie was stunned by the changes she saw in him. The lover she'd left behind had been a college boy who sulked easily and appeared to have no sense of direction. This new Ted was sophisticated and urbane, an honors graduate with an apparently bright future ahead of him. When he asked her to visit him in Seattle, she gladly agreed. There he impressed her with a dinner invitation to Republican chairman Davis' house, then whisked her off to the Davis' condo in Alpental, to ski the slopes they'd visited during their earlier relationship. He impressed her with his ambitious plans for a political career and hinted that he'd never stopped loving her during their time apart. He made no mention of his relationship with Liz Kloepfer, so when he started talking marriage, Stephanie was more than willing to listen.

Stephanie Brooks, of course, had no idea that she was being played. Throughout the rest of 1973, Ted continued to wine and dine her, drawing her ever deeper into his snare. Then, during another of Stephanie's visits to Seattle, he dropped the blade. "I just don't think it's going to work out for us," he told her.

Stephanie was stunned. What had brought about this sudden change of heart? Ted refused to elaborate, saying vaguely that there was another woman involved and that he couldn't "get loose" of her because she'd had an abortion on account of him. When Stephanie tried to discuss it further, he cut her off, launching instead into a rant about his family. He did not even drive her to the airport when she left to return to California on January 2, 1974.

Back on home soil, Stephanie tried to sift through the wreckage, tried to determine what had gone wrong. Was it something she had said or done? She didn't think so. What then? What had come over the man she loved? She waited in vain for a call or a letter, something by way of an explanation. When none came, she decided to consult a therapist, to try and make sense of her feelings. He, in turn, advised her to write to Ted, to ask for an answer. That letter was sent but brought no reply. Eventually, in mid-February, a distraught Stephanie phoned Ted and demanded to know what had brought about his change of heart. His reply was a single sentence. "Stephanie, I have no idea what you mean." Then he hung up on her.

Stephanie Brooks would never speak to Ted Bundy again, although she would hear and read plenty about him. And while that abruptly curtailed phone call left her heartbroken in February 1974, she would be eternally grateful for it in years to come.

Bundy with Stephanie Brooks

Chapter 4: The Entity

It is easy to assume that Ted Bundy lived an entirely normal life during the four years from 1970 to 1974. After all, he was completing an honors degree in psychology, he was beginning his law studies, he held a high-powered job in the Republican Party, he was dating not one, but two women, keeping them secret from one another. There seems hardly to have been enough time for anything else. But Bundy's life during that time was anything but normal. In fact, Ted's treatment of Stephanie Brooks is easily understood if you consider his remarkable ability to compartmentalize different areas of his life. Nowhere is this more evident than in the years of his early to mid-twenties.

Essentially, what you are dealing with are two distinct facets of the same personality. On the one hand there is the brilliant student, the rising politico, the caring voice on the other end of the helpline, the savior of drowning toddlers. On the other is an altogether more malignant persona, wandering the streets at night, peeking into windows, sometimes even following women through the darkened streets, not attacking yet but certainly thinking about it. By day, you'd find him taking outrageous risks as he nurtured his shoplifting obsession. On one occasion, he stole a television set right out of the display window of a department store, in front of several onlookers. On another, he pilfered a six-foot tall potted plant from a nursery, hauling the heavy item to his VW Bug and positioning it on the passenger seat with the top protruding through the sunroof. An arrest in any of these (or several other) instances would have spelled the end of his burgeoning political career but Bundy just did not seem to care. He was gripped by a compulsion that was impossible to fend off, even if he needed to down several beers before embarking on one of his shoplifting expeditions.

And the same applied to his nightly sojourns around the neighborhood. He found that he needed a considerable amount of 'Dutch Courage,' before he could go creeping through the dark, visiting those homes where he knew that drapes were sometimes carelessly left open. Then he began disabling cars, hovering nearby and hoping to present himself as a 'knight in shining armor' to some stranded female motorist. Unfortunately for Bundy, there were always plenty of pedestrians around to come to the woman's aid. And so Bundy tried a different tack. He started following lone women after they left the bars where he routinely drank, the Sandpiper and Dante's, the Pipeline and O'Bannion's. Usually, he kept his distance, tried to find out where the woman lived and hoped that he might catch a peek into her bedroom. But then came the night when he followed a woman with the express intention of attacking her.

The date of this incident is telling, coming just weeks after Bundy ended his relationship with Stephanie. He had just left a bar and had spotted the woman walking along a darkened stretch of sidewalk. Suddenly, he'd been almost overwhelmed with the desire to cause her harm. Had he been sober, he might have questioned this profane urge, any sane person would. But Ted Bundy was a fair distance beyond sober and anyway, the compulsion he now felt was not entirely foreign to him. He'd been fantasizing about it for a long, long time.

Casting around for a weapon, he spotted a piece of two-by-four near a dumpster and snatched it up. Then he set off into the night after his quarry. For several blocks he tracked her, hanging back and keeping to the shadows lest she turn around and spot him grasping his makeshift club. Realizing that he was not going to be able to approach from behind without being seen, he decided on another plan. He cut through an alleyway, sprinted ahead, came up in front of her and crouched in the shadows, waiting. Here she came now. He shifted his grip on the club, licked at his lips with a tongue that was as dry as parchment. Half a block, no one else around. Perfect.

But then the woman veered off the sidewalk and climbed the steps to one of the houses flanking the road. One minute she was there in his sights, the next she was gone, off the street and safe behind a locked door. His prey had escaped. Casting the piece of two-by-four aside in disgust, Bundy staggered off home.

The following morning Bundy awoke nursing a hangover. He remembered the events of the previous evening only vaguely but what he did recall both terrified and excited him. He had fully intended to club an innocent woman with a chunk of wood, perhaps even to kill her. Would he have gone through with it? He knew that he would have. He'd lived with the fantasy for too long to have pulled out when the time came. That evening he was back on the streets hunting again. And he was out again the next evening, and the next. Eventually, on the third night, he encountered a woman fumbling with her car keys on the sidewalk. Her back was turned to him so he ran up silently behind her, raised his club and brought it crashing down onto the back of her head. He thought that he'd applied enough force to knock her out but she hit the ground and then started screaming. Bundy, in terror, turned and fled.

In an interview with authors Stephen G. Michaud and Hugh Aynesworth, conducted years later, Bundy would describe what was going on in his mind during this time. Speaking in the third person (so that his admissions could not be considered a confession) he said that there were two personas fighting for dominance over his life. The first was the rational, law abiding self that tried to keep him from attacking women, that was horrified by the attacks but that also resolved to prevent him from being caught. The other (which he called 'the entity') was a malignant force that drove him to the horrific actions he took. In the aftermath of that first attack, the rational self was in control, terrified and disgusted at what he'd done, even entertaining thoughts of suicide. He swore that he would never do anything like it again and for a couple of months he was good to his word. But as the memory of that first attack began to wane, the entity started nagging at him. Before long he was back on the streets, creeping through alleyways and peeping into windows. It was on one of those expeditions that he spotted Karen Sparks in her basement apartment near the UW campus.

On the morning of January 5, 1974, 18-year-old Karen Sparks failed to join her housemates for breakfast. They were not unduly concerned with this as Karen sometimes slept in when she didn't have morning classes. When she still had not put in an appearance by mid-afternoon, however, they began to worry. One of them went down to check on her. The girl immediately noticed that the door to the basement, which was usually locked, stood slightly ajar. Entering the darkened room, she saw Karen lying on the bed, under the covers. It was only when she got closer that she noticed the clotted blood that covered her friend's face and hair.

Someone had gotten into Karen's apartment during the night, wrenched a metal bar from the bedframe and beaten her unconscious with it. The intruder had then rammed the same bar into her vagina, causing terrible internal injuries. She would remain comatose for over a week and would be permanently brain damaged by the attack. But she would survive. The next victim would not.

Lynda Ann Healy

Lynda Ann Healy was a beautiful and accomplished young woman. At the age of 21, she was in her senior year as a psychology major. She hoped, after graduation, to work with mentally handicapped children. Quite aside from her academic achievements, she was a talented singer and a part-time weather reporter on a local radio station. She lived near the UW Campus at 5517 12th N.E., in a house she shared with four other female students. This was just a few blocks away from where Karen Sparks had been attacked four weeks earlier.

On the evening of January 31, 1974, Lynda went with friends for a few beers and a meal at the nearby Dante's Tavern. Dante's was, of course, one of Ted Bundy's favorite hangouts but there is no evidence that he was in the bar that night. He did, however, know about Lynda and her housemates. In fact, he'd been watching them for weeks.

Lynda did not stay long at Dante's that evening. She and her friends were back home in an hour and Lynda then spoke with an old boyfriend on the phone before watching a bit of television and then retiring to her room in the basement. She had an early start in the morning as she had to do the Ski Report at the radio station. She therefore got straight into bed and was soon asleep. A short while later, Ted Bundy, who had been watching the house, waiting for the lights to be extinguished, was at the door leading into Lynda's apartment. He turned the handle speculatively, fully expecting it to be locked. It wasn't. Stealthily, silently, he entered.

The basement room where Lynda Healy lived was divided into two units by a thin plywood wall. Brenda Little, who occupied the other half of the room was used to hearing Lynda's alarm go off at 5:30 each morning. Usually, the alarm was quickly turned off but not today. It kept up its strident tone until Brenda eventually had to go into Lynda's room to turn it off. She found the room neatly arranged with the bed made and nothing that appeared untoward. Lynda, it seemed, had already left for work. Brenda was just about to leave when the telephone started ringing. It was the radio station wondering where Lynda was. Brenda assured them that she was on her way.

No further inquiries were made about Lynda that day. Her housemates were somewhat perplexed when she didn't show up for classes but they assumed that she must have had something important to attend to. It was only when Lynda failed to arrive for dinner at her parents' home that evening that the alarm was raised. Then a quick round of calls determined that no one had seen Lynda in the last 20 hours or so and that the bicycle that she usually rode to the radio station was still outside her room. Within the hour, Lynda had been reported to the Seattle Police as a missing person.

The police were acutely aware that another young girl had been brutally attacked in the same neighborhood less than four weeks earlier, so they wasted little time in dispatching Detectives Wayne Dorman and Ted Fonis to the scene. There, they found Lynda's room as neat and tidy as Brenda Little had described it. Something was off, though, and one of the girls pointed it out to the detectives. It was the way that the bed was made. Lynda was in the habit of pulling the sheet over her pillow. Now it was tucked under.

That is what led the officers to pull back the covers and discover a blotch of dried blood that stained both the sheet and the underside of the pillow. Not enough blood to indicate that anyone had died here but certainly enough to suggest that someone had been seriously injured. One of the bedsheets was also missing. A search of the room then turned up another anomaly. Lynda's nightgown was found hanging in the closet, a ring of dried blood around the neckline. Lynda's friends also pointed out that the clothes she'd worn the previous evening were gone.

The detectives had by now been able to piece together a troubling theory of what had happened to Lynda Healy. It appeared that someone had entered Lynda's apartment during the night, subdued her, possibly with a blow to the head, then stripped off her nightgown, dressed her in street clothes and carried her away, wrapped in a bedsheet. That, at least, seemed to indicate that Lynda was alive when she was taken and might still be.

She wasn't though. After carrying Lynda unconscious from her apartment, Bundy had loaded her into his VW Bug and driven her into the mountains, close to the slopes that he and Stephanie had so loved to ski. There, he'd dragged her unconscious from his car, undressed her, raped her, and sodomized her. He would continue to sexually abuse the terrified woman after she regained consciousness, keeping up his assault until the first light of dawn began to temper the darkness, ignoring all of his victim's pleas. Finally, he'd strangled her. He would commit other atrocities on the body but those would only come to light much later.

Bundy had driven away both exhilarated and fearful. The murder had filled some primal need in him, satisfied some deep-seated compulsion. But he was also terrified that someone might have seen him entering Lynda Healy's apartment, or carrying her body away from the scene. He felt certain that he'd soon feel the harsh grip of John Law on his collar. In the weeks that followed, he tracked the course of the police investigation in the newspapers and his tension eased as he realized that they had nothing on him. Then he began prowling again as the needs of 'the entity' took precedence.

Ted Bundy would later ascribe surprising roles to the two personas that governed his existence. He said that 'the entity' was driven by the need to abduct and sexually violate young women while his 'normal self' was responsible for the murders which (at least initially) were committed to eliminate the possibility of the victim testifying against him. He was quick to stress that he was not describing a 'split personality' but rather distinctive aspects of himself, each of which may have held sway at different times. After each of the initial murders, the 'normal self' would assert control and insist that this would never happen again. However, the passage of time would lessen his resistance and the entity would re-emerge, forcing him to go hunting.

What Bundy was describing is a pattern of behavior observed in all serial killers – a murder, followed by a cooling down period, followed by another murder. Often the killer accelerates, with less and less time between kills. So it was with Ted Bundy.

On the rainy Tuesday evening of March 12, 1974, 19-year-old Donna Manson set off from her dorm room at Evergreen State College near Olympia, Washington. Her destination was a jazz concert that was being held on campus that night but somewhere between her room and the concert hall, she vanished. Donna was not immediately reported missing since she was known to be a free spirit, prone to hit the road at a moment's notice, returning later with no explanation as to where she'd been. It was six days before anyone thought to contact the authorities. Then a search radiated out from the university campus hoping to find some trace of her. There was none. Donna had long since taken her last ride into the mountains in the backseat of Ted Bundy's VW. Given the long distance between the site of her abduction and that of Lynda Healy, the crimes were not initially linked. That, of course, was exactly as Bundy had intended.

For his next murder, Bundy ventured even further afield, over the Cascade Mountains to the town of Ellensburg, some 120 miles from Seattle. Susan Rancourt was a freshman at Central Washington State College in the town. Susan was a pretty girl with long blonde hair and sparkling blue eyes. She was a timid soul, described by her friends as being "afraid of her own shadow." She refused, in fact, to be alone outdoors after dark.

But on the evening of April 17, 1974, Susan made an exception to her own rule. The reason for this uncharacteristic behavior was a job. There were some openings for dorm advisors and as she was paying her own way through college she needed the money. Interviews were being held that evening and so Susan dumped a load of washing at the dorm laundromat and then set off across campus to the advisors' meeting. That meeting was over by nine, after which Susan was due to meet a friend to watch a movie. It was a movie she would never see. Sometime after leaving the meeting, Susan Rancourt had the misfortune of encountering Ted Bundy. Susan was trained in karate but at five-foot-two she would have stood no chance against the six-foot Bundy, especially as he was armed with his favored means of destruction, a tire iron.

Chapter 5: Taken in the Night

Susan Rancourt was reported missing the following day, when she failed to return to her dorm and her load of washing was discovered in the washer where she'd left it the previous evening. The campus police immediately launched a search for her and then called the Sherriff's department when that search proved fruitless. As deputies began questioning students, the first clues began to emerge. One girl told of encountering a tall, handsome man who had his arm in a sling. He appeared to be having trouble carrying his pile of books and asked her if she'd mind helping him to his car. She agreed but as she approached the vehicle, a brownish VW Bug, she noticed that the passenger seat was missing. That, for some reason, spooked her, causing her hair to stand on end. She'd no sooner place the books on the hood of the car than she turned and sprinted away. Another young woman told a remarkably similar story about an encounter with the same man. The police, however, did not consider this a viable lead. Nerves were understandably frayed over Susan Rancourt's mysterious disappearance. At times like these even the most mundane of incidents could be made to appear sinister.

But the disappearances of three young college students and the brutal attack on a fourth were causing alarm. Already there were whisperings that despite the distances between the crimes they might be connected. Some of those whisperings made their way into the press and inevitably Ted Bundy got to read about them. He, after all, was following the stories of the missing girls more closely than anyone. Partly this was to keep track of what the police knew and didn't know, partly it was for his own amusement. What imbeciles the police were, running around in circles like the Keystone Cops. They were way off the mark. They had, however, picked up a pattern to the crimes, something that Bundy had been desperate to avoid. For his next killing, he went out of state.

Roberta "Kathy" Parks

Roberta "Kathy" Parks was a student at Oregon State University, although she was finding it hard to settle and pining for her home in Lafayette, California. Kathy had good reason to be homesick, her father had recently suffered a heart attack and she was worried about him. For a time, she'd considered dropping everything and heading home to be by his side. But now, two days later, she had better news from her sister. Her father's condition had stabilized and he was on the mend. Somewhat relieved, Kathy agreed to meet up with friends for coffee at the Student Union Building. She left her dorm room in the early evening and promptly disappeared.

This time there were no sightings of mysterious men on campus. In fact, foul play was not suspected at first. Given Kathy's recent state of mind, it was feared that she might have taken her own life. But if that were the case, where was her body? The Willamette River was dragged and provided no answer. Kathy had vanished without a trace. Was her disappearance linked to those of the other girls? Law officers were divided on the issue but most thought not. Oregon State was just too far away from the epicenter of events in Seattle.

But once again, the police had underestimated the fortitude of the man they were hunting. Ted Bundy had not only driven to Oregon to abduct a victim he'd driven that victim all the way back to Washington to murder her. The Parks murder was different to most of the others in that Bundy had not forcibly abducted Kathy, he'd talked her into accompanying him. He'd encountered Kathy in the Student Union cafeteria waiting for her friends to arrive. As a psychology graduate, as someone who'd worked the Seattle Crisis hotline for months, he had picked up right away that she was depressed. He'd struck up a conversation with her, pushing all the right buttons, saying the things he knew would win her trust. When he'd asked her to go with him for a drink, she'd willingly agreed.

Instead of driving to a bar as he'd suggested, though, Bundy headed out of town. Kathy must have become increasingly anxious as the lights of the city slipped behind them. Before she could protest, Bundy abruptly brought the car to a stop beside a cornfield and ordered her out. Then he told her to undress.

Kathy Parks could not have known that she was caught out in the middle of nowhere with a man who had already murdered three young women in the most horrific way. She probably realized that she was about to be raped and likely chastised herself for getting into a car with a complete stranger. Nonetheless, she was determined to live through this night and so she offered no resistance as Bundy ravished her and then told her to get dressed and ordered her back into the car. She probably expected him to drop her off on some remote stretch of road far from a phone, allowing him to make his getaway. He didn't. Instead, he drove her all the way to Washington, into the foothills of the Cascades. There he again ordered her from the vehicle and told her to walk ahead of him into the brush. Did Kathy Parks spot the bones of Bundy's earlier victims as he marched her to his favored killing ground on Taylor Mountain? Did she catch the whiff of carrion? We don't know. All we know is that she died terrified and alone and that her decapitated head would later be discovered on that spot.

There is a common misconception about serial killer M.O.'s, the belief being that they find a method that works and stick to it no matter what. Nothing could be further from the truth. This type of killer is always learning, always refining and improving his methods. What remains unchanged is the killer's signature, those ritualistic behaviors that he feels compelled to repeat time and again.

Ted Bundy was a particularly inventive killer who switched readily between ruse and force in luring or subduing his victims. His signature, however, remained constant. Like many emerging serial killers, Bundy most likely did not understand his motivation when he committed his early crimes. By his own admission, his purpose was sexual assault and the victims were killed solely to cover up that crime. At least, that is what he initially believed.

But he soon came to realize that his motive was far more primal than that. He called it 'possession,' and what stronger manifestation of your ability to possess another human being than to take that person's life? After the first few murders, the desire to 'possess' became his motive. The sexual assault, the thrill of the hunt, everything else became supplementary. Bundy, in fact, quickly devolved to an almost primordial level of depravity in how he dealt with his victims. His contention has always been that he dispatched them quickly to avoid unnecessary pain and suffering. That is untrue. He undoubtedly got off on their mental anguish and if he restrained himself from torturing them physically, that was only because he preferred an inanimate sex partner to a living one.

Bundy was a necrophile. Evidence exists that he visited his dump sites time and again to have sex with the decomposing corpses. There is also evidence that he decapitated some of his victims and carried their heads home with him where he applied make-up, washed their hair and undoubtedly used them as sex toys. (Similar behavior has been noted in other serial killers including Douglas Clark, Ed Kemper and Jerome Brudos). The point is that Bundy had evolved into an altogether more dangerous beast over the first few months of his murderous career. He had come to crave the act of murder itself. And his killing spree was gaining momentum.

Twenty-six days after the murder of Roberta Parks, he struck
again.

Brenda Ball was 22 years old and shared a house with two other
girls in the suburb of Burien, Washington. On the evening of May
31, 1974, Brenda told her housemates that she was going to a
popular local bar called the Flame Tavern. Brenda was seen at the
Flame that night and remained until closing time at around 2 a.m.
By then she was fairly intoxicated. She asked one of the other
patrons for a lift home but the man said that he was going in the
opposite direction. Shrugging, Brenda walked to the curbside and
stuck out her thumb. A short while later a VW Bug stopped to give
her a ride. The man at the wheel was Ted Bundy.

We only know what happened to Brenda Ball because of Bundy's
later description of the crime. He said that he'd started talking to
her and asked if she wanted to go to a party at his house. Brenda
agreed and he'd driven her to the house where he was staying. If
Brenda was alarmed that the place was in darkness and that there
was quite obviously no party in progress, she made no protest.
Once inside, she and Bundy continued drinking and started
making out. Eventually, they had consensual sex which Bundy
found unfulfilling. He had much darker desires than that.

Brenda was by now quite drunk and she eventually passed out,
leaving Bundy with an easy kill. After strangling her, he sexually
violated her corpse. Then he pushed her into a closet and went to
sleep. Brenda Ball's corpse would remain in Bundy's bedroom for
several days, until the smell of decomposition forced him to drive
her into the mountains, to one of his regular dumping grounds.

Given what we know of Bundy's tastes we can be certain that he continued to act out perversions on the corpse during that time.

Brenda Ball

Like Donna Manson, Brenda Ball had been a free spirit, prone to taking off on some or other adventure at a moment's notice and without telling anyone where she was headed. Her disappearance therefore caused no alarm at first. However, when two weeks passed with no word from Brenda, her roommates began to worry. Brenda had taken none of her clothes and she'd drawn no money from her bank account during that time. Eventually, after 19 days with no word from Brenda, her friends went to the police and reported her missing. By that time Ted Bundy was already out trawling for his next victim. He was about to pull off his most audacious crime yet.

During the early part of his killing spree, Bundy had been mindful
that the disappearances of several young women would spark a
rigorous response from the police. He had tried to temper this by
traveling as far as Oregon in search of victims and by trying to vary
his victim type. (Brenda Ball, for example, was slightly older than
the other girls and was not a student). But Bundy's attempts at
subterfuge were in vain. Most law enforcement officers in King
County and beyond, now attributed the disappearances to a single
perpetrator. Bundy, of course, knew this from following the case in
the media, knew that it was pointless continuing the ruse. On
Monday, June 10, he returned to his favored hunting ground, the
area around the University of Washington campus.

Georgann Hawkins

Georgann Hawkins was 5-foot-two inches tall, 115 pounds and pretty with long brown hair, lively brown eyes and pixie-like features. The 18-year-old was a straight A student save for the one subject that kept her up at night. With a final exam coming in Spanish, Georgann planned to spend the night of June 10 cramming.

Not everyone who lived in the frat houses that lined "Greek Row" (17th Avenue N.E.) was as diligent. There was a party that night which Georgann attended with friends early in the evening, although she soon cried off and said she had to get back to her sorority house to study. First, though, she was going to stop off at her boyfriend's residence for a brief visit.

Georgann was generally a cautious girl, made more so by the recent disappearances of female students from Washington campuses. But the route she had to walk along Greek Row was well-lit and busy, with lots of students milling about. All of the houses had bedrooms facing the street and virtually every light was on, with students pulling all-nighters in the run-up to finals. Georgann would have passed these windows on route to her boyfriend's room in Beta House. By the time she left him at 12:40 not much had changed on the street, most of the lights were still on, there were still people around, the strains of music could still be heard from the party. As Georgann walked past one of the houses, a male friend stuck his head out of a window and shouted a friendly greeting which Georgann returned with a wave and a smile. Georgann Hawkins had just forty, well-lit feet to walk to her home at Theta House. She never made it.

Georgann's roommate, Dee Williams had been waiting up for her, waiting to hear the rattle of pebbles on her window pane, a pre-arranged signal that Georgann was downstairs and wanted to be let in (Georgann had recently lost her keys). But the signal never came. An hour passed. Two hours. Eventually, a concerned Dee phoned Georgann's boyfriend only to learn that she'd left hours earlier. Dee then ran to wake the house mother and the police were called.

The Seattle Police threw everything they had at the inexplicable disappearance of Georgann Hawkins, even calling in the help of renowned criminalist George Ishii. But despite a search of the area by detectives who covered Georgann's route on hands and knees, there was not one single clue to suggest what had happened to her. (Years later, it would emerge that Bundy returned to the crime scene on the morning after the murder. While detectives were scampering around looking for clues, Bundy was in the crowd behind the yellow crime scene tape, watching).

Georgann's sorority sisters were questioned, of course. But no of them had seen or heard anything. Not a scream, not a sound. There were, however, some interesting reports from two other students. One of the girls said that she had been walking along 17th N.E. at around 12:30 when she'd spotted a tall man hobbling along on crutches. His jeans leg was torn along the seam to accommodate the cast he wore. He was carrying a briefcase which he kept dropping. As the girl passed, the man asked if she could help him by carrying the case to his car. She said that she would but first had to go into one of the houses. She was longer in the house than expected and when she eventually came out the man was gone. Whatever had delayed her, had likely saved her life.

The second report came from a male student who said that he'd seen the same man hobbling along on crutches. There was a girl walking beside him, carrying a briefcase. Shown a picture of Georgann Hawkins the student was adamant that it had not been her. These stories, of course, were very similar to the ones reported after Susan Rancourt's disappearance but they got the police no closer to unraveling the mystery.

So what had happened to Georgann? It seems likely that she was attacked in the alleyway beside her sorority house, which she would have had to enter in order to attract Dee Williams' attention. This thoroughfare is as brightly-lit as the street but it is screened from general view. It is here that Ted Bundy waited. Georgann was short-sighted and was wearing neither her glasses nor contact lenses that night. That would have allowed Bundy to get close to her before she perceived any danger. He might even have called to her by name, having heard her male acquaintance use it just moments earlier. Thereafter, a swift blow to the head would have rendered her unconscious and he would have carried her back to his waiting Bug. Whatever the case, Georgann Hawkins was gone, taken in the night. Her body would never be found.

Homicide investigations are all about building links. Links between victim and suspect, links between one victim and another. More often than not, these links are what point the police in the direction of the killer. But in a serial murder investigation these steps hardly ever produce a break. Serial killers target complete strangers and there is usually nothing that connects the victims, one to another. There is a preferred victim type certainly and in this case the killer appeared to be seeking out attractive and accomplished young women. Many of the victims even resembled one another with long, dark-brown hair parted in the middle. (It has been noted that these girls looked a lot like Stephanie Brooks, Ted Bundy's former fiancée.)

Still, the Seattle police tried to connect the victims by something more than their physical characteristics. They brought in Karen Sparks, the only victim thus far who was known to have escaped the Co-Ed Killer. Karen was shown photographs of the missing girls – Lynda, Donna, Susan, Kathy, Brenda, Georgann – and asked if she knew any of them. She said no, effectively cutting off that avenue of investigation.

In the meanwhile, the story of the missing Co-Eds continued to dominate the media, throwing Washingtonians into a state of panic. Women stayed off the streets at night and seldom walked alone during the daytime; windows that had once been left open were now securely bolted; new locks were fitted to doors; there was a drastic drop-off in the number of female hitchhikers. Ted Bundy would have observed all of this with barely concealed glee. The panic he was causing would most definitely have appealed to his narcissistic personality. But that panic also left him with a problem. His potential victims were now on full alert, jumping at shadows and ready to bolt at the first sign of danger. His solution? Hit them when they least expect it. Like in broad daylight, on a crowded beach, at a popular resort.

Chapter 6: Lake Sammamish

Lake Sammamish lies some twelve miles east of Seattle along Interstate 90. It is a popular resort drawing large crowds from Seattle and its satellite towns during the hot days of summer. July 14, 1974 was just such a day, with the temperature headed towards a rare 90 degrees. 40,000 people would head for the lakeshore on that glorious day, among them a pretty blonde named Janice Ott. Janice was a tiny woman, who stood just over five-feet tall and weighed in at around 100 pounds. She looked more like a high school student than her actual age of 23.

At around 12:30 that morning, Janice was sun tanning on the beach at Lake Sammamish when she was approached by a young man. He was tall and handsome, dressed in white shorts, a white tennis shirt and sneakers, and wearing a cast on his arm. He fixed her with a friendly smile. "Say," he said. "You wouldn't mind lending me a hand, would you?"

Janice regarded the man through her sunglasses, noticed the cast on his arm and decided that he appeared non-threatening. "Sure," she said. "What do you need?"

"I need some help loading my sailboat onto my car," the man said. "I'd do it myself, only…" He broke off in mid-sentence and held up his arm, indicating the cast.

Janice again did a quick computation while the man looked on sheepishly. He was well-mannered and well-spoken and did not seem in the least bit dangerous. Besides, he was disabled and surely he wouldn't have approached her on a crowded beach if he meant her any harm?

"How about you sit down awhile and we talk about it," Janice said. "I'm Jan, by the way."

"Ted," the man said, easing himself to the sand beside her. He then went on to explain that the boat was at his parents' house just a short distance down the road in Issaquah.

"Issaquah?" Janice said, "That's where I live too. The thing is, I cycled here this morning and I don't want to leave my bike unattended."

"No problem," Ted said, "we'll put it in the trunk of my car."

"Okay, I'll help you," Janet said after a moment's reflection. "Only you'll have to give me a ride on your boat when you get it here."

"Done deal!" Ted replied.

Minutes later, other beachgoers saw Janice walking beside the man with the cast, pushing her bike in the direction of a metallic brown VW bug. She was never seen alive again.

At around 4 p.m. that afternoon, the man who'd called on Janice Ott's assistance approached another woman with a similar proposition. The woman agreed to help but cried off when the man asked her to accompany him to his parents' house. At 4:15, the same man approached yet another female beachgoer but something about him made her suspicious and she said that she had people waiting for her and couldn't spare the time. He then thanked her courteously and walked off in the direction of the restrooms. A short while later, the woman saw him in conversation with a pretty, dark-haired girl of around 18.

Janice Ott (left) and Denise Naslund

Denise Naslund had come to the lake that day in the company of
her boyfriend and another young couple. They'd all driven there in
Denise's 1963 Chevy. The quartet had spent the day swimming
and sunbathing and at around four had roasted some hotdogs. At
4:30, Denise had said that she was going to the bathroom and had
walked off in the direction of the cinderblock building near the
parking lot that housed those facilities. When she still had not
returned half an hour later, her friends began to get worried and
went looking for her. That search would become ever more frantic
as the day waned into dusk. Eventually, with the parking lot
thinning out and Denise's car still standing where she'd parked it,
her friends tracked down a park ranger and reported her missing.
It was now 8:30 p.m. Denise Naslund had been gone for four hours,
Janice Ott for twice that long.

The following day, the King County Sherriff's Department
launched a massive, but ultimately fruitless, search for Denise
Naslund. They did not even know that Janice Ott was missing until
her husband, who had been working away in California, reported
that he'd been unable to reach his wife for several days.

The story of what happened to Janice Ott and Denise Naslund is
perhaps the most harrowing of the entire Bundy saga. We know it,
once again, because of the curious "third person confession" that
Bundy gave to authors Michaud and Aynesworth.

According to Bundy, the Lake Sammamish abductions were driven
by his desperate need to find another victim. He'd contemplated,

in the past, abducting a woman from a public place but had always dismissed it as too risky. However, by mid-July, his level of stress had built up to such an extent that he needed to alleviate it. The only way he knew how to do that was through murder. On that Sunday morning, he'd heard a radio broadcast, announcing that record crowds were expected at the lake and had decided to go trawling.

Bundy's telling of events is not entirely true. The Lake Sammamish murders were not a spur of the moment thing. He had almost certainly planned them ahead of time. In fact, Bundy had been spotted at the lake in the week prior to the abductions, spotted by some people who knew him through his political activities. He had also scoped out the nearby town of Issaquah, looking for a vacant property to which he could bring his victim. He had found an unoccupied holiday home, broken in, and done the groundwork. Now all he had to do was wait for Sunday, when the lakeshore would be teeming with young women, each a potential target.

Bundy had approached a number of women before Janice Ott made the grave mistake of falling for his cover story. Janice was taken to the house in Issaquah where she was overpowered at knifepoint, tied up and then repeatedly raped and sodomized. Then Bundy left to return to the lake and secure another victim. It had long been a fantasy of his to kill two women together.

Denise Naslund was the unfortunate second woman. Like Janice, she'd fallen for Bundy's story and agreed to accompany him to his "parent's home." There she suffered the same fate as Janice, threatened with a knife, tied up and then sexually assaulted. What makes this crime particularly perverse is that the two girls were assaulted in front of each other. Then one of them was killed while the other was forced to watch. One can only imagine the terror of the surviving victim as she saw the other murdered before her eyes, as she waited helplessly for the killer to turn his deadly attentions on her.

Ted Bundy, as we have already seen, was obsessed with possessing his victims' bodies. Wherever he could, he held onto the corpses, concealed in his room. In this case, however, he had no idea when the owner of the property might return. And so, Janice Ott and Denise Naslund were driven into the mountains that same evening. By the time the search was launched the following morning, they were already lying, exposed to the elements, in one of Ted Bundy's makeshift graveyards.

The dreadful events at Lake Sammamish on that July afternoon had sparked a renewed media frenzy. Reporters now had a name to latch on to. Several witnesses had heard the abductor introduce himself to Janice Ott as "Ted." Was it his real name? Investigators thought not. If, as it appeared, he'd come to the lake intent on abducting a girl, he was hardly likely to have given his name. Still, the possibility existed that he had done just that.

What interested the police more was a description. Ted had been seen by several witnesses. He'd approached a number of women with his sailboat story. All but Janice and Denise had rebuffed him for one reason or another. In each of these instances, he'd accepted the rejection graciously and quickly moved on to the next woman. From the descriptions that some of these potential victims provided, a consistent picture began to emerge – tall, slim, good-looking, perhaps mid-twenties, hair neatly cut, sandy brown in color and slightly wavy, well-spoken with an unusual accent, perhaps British, perhaps Canadian. These inputs went to a police sketch artist who was able to compile a composite. That, in turn, was rushed to the media. Soon a picture of the mysterious Ted was decorating the front page of every newspaper in King County and glaring down from police posters plastered around the area.

This, of course, triggered a deluge of clues and tip-offs, so many that the Seattle police department was unable to cope and had to have a payroll computer reprogrammed to process the data. It seemed that just about everyone knew someone who looked like the "Ted" in the composite sketch and drove a Bug. And there were a number of people who thought that he resembled Ted Bundy.

One of them was an up-and-coming true crime author named Ann Rule, who had worked with Bundy at the Seattle Crisis Center. Rule mentioned her suspicion to Seattle Homicide Detective Dick Reed who noted that Bundy drove a bronze-colored VW Bug. However, Rule never believed at that stage that Ted Bundy was the "Ted" in the picture and neither did the Seattle Police Department. Bundy was just one name on their list of 2,400 suspects and he hardly fit the profile of a mass murderer. He was an honors graduate after all, with connections to the Governor. (Ann Rule would, of course, go on to become a bestselling author and would write one of the definitive accounts of the Bundy case.)

Another woman who suspected Ted Bundy was Lynn Banks, a close friend of Bundy's girlfriend, Liz Kloepfer. Banks, in fact, confronted Liz on several occasions, thrust the newspaper in front of her, and challenged her to deny that the sketch looked like Ted.

Liz admitted that there was a resemblance, admitted that Ted did drive a Bug like the one described in the articles. But she refused to believe that Ted could have had anything to do with the disappearances. She was dealing with her own issues at the time. Ted had called in his earlier acceptance to the University of Utah law school and was about to depart for Salt Lake City. Liz was afraid that she might lose him forever.

Chapter 7: The Worst We Feared Is True

While the hunt for the Co-Ed killer continued, the man that the Seattle police were so desperately seeking slipped quietly out of Washington State on Labor Day weekend 1974. Ted Bundy was driving a pick-up, towing his VW behind him. He got out of town just before the police made their first real break in the case. On September 8, a couple of grouse hunters were walking through the brush about two miles east of Lake Sammamish National Park when they chanced upon what appeared to be a partial human skeleton – a lower jaw, a rib cage and a complete spinal column.

King County deputies were quickly on the scene and arrived just in time to cordon off the area and prevent TV crews from trampling evidence into the ground. A grid search was then carried out, one that would endure for four days and turn up more bones, including a second skull, five thigh bones and tufts of human hair. Time, scavengers and the elements had seen to it that there was nothing more for the investigators to find but it was clear that the victims had been nude when their bodies were so callously discarded. There was no clothing found at the site, no pieces of jewelry or other items.

The grim task of identifying the victims fell to UW Anthropology professor, Dr. Darus Swindler. Dental charts and hair samples assisted him in this task and a few days later the police called a press conference and made the announcement that everyone was dreading. "The worst we feared is true," Captain Nick Mackie said.

"We have identified the remains of Janice Ott and Denise Naslund."
What Mackie didn't say was that the thigh bones found at the site
indicated four different victims. It was impossible, from the
remains, to identify the other two.

An expanded search was planned to hunt for the skulls of the other
victims but by now, the first snows of winter had fallen in the
Cascades Mountains and the search had to be put off until the
spring. In the meantime, a task force comprising officers of the
Seattle PD and King County Sherriff's department set up shop in
the county courthouse building and began revisiting every scrap of
evidence they had on the elusive Ted. They had no idea that the
subject of their search was 800 miles away, preparing to begin his
law classes at the University of Utah. Those classes had barely
begun when the plague that had been visited upon the female
population in Washington, started up anew.

On September 2, Bundy picked up a hitchhiker in Idaho, raped and
strangled her and then dumped her body in the woods, returning
the following day to photograph the corpse and dismember it.
That victim has never been identified. On October 2, he snatched
16-year-old Nancy Wilcox from a street in Holladay, Utah, drove
her to a wooded area and there raped and murdered her. Bundy
would later claim that he had not intended killing Nancy and that
he'd accidentally suffocated her while trying to stifle her screams.
Given what we know of the depraved killer, that is difficult to
believe. Nancy Wilcox was buried near Capitol Reef National Park,
some 200 miles south of Holladay. No one connected the murder
to Bundy until he confessed to it years later.

Melissa Smith

On the evening of Friday, October 18, 1974, a pretty 17-year-old named Melissa Smith was preparing to attend a slumber party at a friend's home. Melissa's father was the police chief of Midvale, a small town of some 5,000 residents, just south of Salt Lake City. As the daughter of a law officer, Melissa was probably more vigilant than the average teenager. It had been drilled into her from childhood.

Melissa had not yet left for her sleepover when she received a call from another friend who was tearful and distressed after a fight with her boyfriend. This friend worked at a nearby Pizza parlor and Melissa agreed to stop by to talk to her before setting off for the party. It was by now already 9:30 p.m. and her route would take her along a dirt road, under a railway bridge and across a school playground. Still, Melissa wasn't concerned. Midvale was a

quiet town and most of its citizens were churchgoing Mormons.
Crime was rare here and violent crime almost unheard of.

Melissa Smith would not have known of the monster who had
recently moved down from Seattle. She made it safely to the Pizza
parlor and spent a half-hour commiserating with her friend before
heading back home. Her homeward journey would have taken her
along the same path. Somewhere along that path she encountered
Ted Bundy. It would be nine days before her brutalized body was
found, in the Wasatch Mountains, east of Salt Lake City. She had
been severely beaten, sustaining fractures to her skull and massive
hemorrhages to her brain. She had also been strangled with her
own stocking. Before that, she'd been raped and sodomized. Bundy
would later admit that he'd visited the corpse several times in the
days after the murder, to wash its hair and apply makeup.

The Melissa Smith murder investigation was assigned to Detective
Jerry Thompson of the Salt Lake County Sherriff's Department. But
he'd barely got started when another young woman went missing.
On Halloween night, October 31, 1974, 17-year-old Laura Aime
walked away from a diner in Lehi, Utah and promptly disappeared.
Her body was found 27 days later, on a river bank in the Wasatch
Mountains. She was naked, her face so badly battered that she
could only be identified by an old scar on her forearm, the result of
a childhood horse riding accident. As in the case of Melissa Smith,
Laura had been raped and sodomized. And the pathologist was
able to determine the type of weapon that had been used to kill
her. She had been beaten to death with a crowbar.

The detectives still hunting for 'Ted' back in Seattle would have known nothing about these murders. In the modern era, of course, the details would be entered into the FBI's VICAP (Violent Criminal Apprehension Program) computer and a link would quickly be made. But back in 1974, the system did not exist leading to what investigators call "linkage blindness," where detectives in different jurisdictions are hunting the same man but unaware of each other's activities.

One person, however, did make the link between the Washington and Utah killings. Lynn Banks, friend of Bundy's girlfriend Liz Kloepfer, had long suspected Ted of being the Co-Ed Killer, had, in fact, urged Liz to report him to the police. During the Fall of 1974, Lynn made a trip home to Utah and read about the two murdered teenagers. She was stunned by the similarities. The girls looked so similar to the Washington victims and they'd been bludgeoned to death with a crowbar, just like Janice Ott and Denise Naslund.

When she returned to Washington, Lynn carried the newspaper cuttings with her and showed them to Liz. "You know it's him," she said. "You have to go to the police. You can't keep covering for him."

Eventually, Liz Kloepfer did contact the King County Sherriff's office but she resented Lynn for making her give them Ted's name and it ended their friendship. Ted Bundy's name was duly entered into the task force's primitive computer, the fourth time it had been logged.

Chapter 8: Survivor

Bundy, of course, had no idea that Liz had spoken to the police. On the rainy Friday evening of November 8, 1974. He was out hunting again, cruising the Fashion Place Shopping Mall in Murray, Utah. Eighteen-year-old Carol DaRonch, newly graduated from high school, had come to the mall that night in her new Camaro, arriving a little before seven. She'd done some shopping, chatted with friends and was browsing through a magazine at Walden's Book Store when a man approached her. He asked if she'd parked her car near the Sear's store and she said that she had. He then asked for her license plate number and nodded as she repeated it. Someone had been caught trying to break into the car, he said. Would she mind accompanying him out to the parking lot to see if anything had been stolen?

Carol, assuming that the man must be a security guard or a police officer, agreed. But as they left the well-lit corridors of the mall and stepped into the relative gloom of the parking lot, she began to have second thoughts. How had this man known that she was the owner of the Camaro? How had he known where to find her? Somewhat apprehensive now she asked to see his identification. The man however, dismissed her request with a chuckle and she felt foolish for having asked. They were at the car anyway, so she opened the driver's door and quickly ascertained that nothing had been taken. The man then asked her to open the passenger door as well but she refused, saying that she was certain that nothing was missing. Now the man insisted that she accompany him to the police substation in the mall. His partner was there, he said, and likely had the thief in custody.

Carol DaRonch

By now, Carol's apprehension had given way to a certain amount of tetchiness. She had no idea why any of this was necessary when it was obvious that her car had not been broken into. Still, she followed the man when he walked off at pace, rounded the outside of the building and rapped on a door marked with the number 139. When no one answered the knock he told her that his partner had probably taken the suspect to the station and said that she would have to go there with him to sign a statement. Carol said that she would drive there in her own car but the man insisted that she would have to come with him in his. That turned out to be a battered VW Bug.

Now Carol really was concerned. The Bug did not look like any police vehicle she'd ever seen. Again she insisted on seeing some ID and this time the man reluctantly complied, flashing a small gold shield and saying that he was "Officer Roseland" of the Murray PD. Her fears still not entirely allayed, Carol got into the passenger seat of the VW.

But she soon had reason to regret that decision. "Officer Roseland" headed the Bug in the opposite direction to the police station. When Carol pointed that out to him, he gunned the engine and raced off into the night. Along a darkened stretch of road, in front of the McMillan Grade School, he suddenly slammed on the brakes.

Carol, already poised for flight, grabbed for the door handle. But she hadn't got it open yet when she felt a vice-like grip on her arm and heard a click. He'd clapped a handcuff on her wrist.

If Carol had harbored any doubt before, she had none now. This man meant to kill her. She was in a fight for her life. She started screaming, lashing out with her nails as the man tried to cuff her other hand. Such were her struggles that when he eventually succeeded in getting the cuffs on her, he closed both of them on the same wrist. Then, as she continued to scream, to reach behind her in an effort to open the door, she saw that he was holding a gun. "Keep screaming," he said. "And I'll blow your brains out." At that moment the door finally swung open and Carol spilled out of the car backwards onto the wet sidewalk. She was still struggling to her feet when the man rounded the car and came at her, holding a crowbar.

But for the adrenaline surging through her veins, Carol DaRonch might well have died there on the wet sidewalk in front of the McMillan School. But with a strength born of her desperation to survive, she threw up a hand, deflected his blow and then forced her knee up into his groin. The man let out a grunt and hunched over and then Carol was free of him and sprinting into the darkness. Behind her, she could hear his footfalls pounding the sidewalk. He was closing. He was going to catch her.

But where luck had deserted every unfortunate woman that Ted Bundy had targeted thus far, it would smile kindly on Carol DaRonch. A pair of headlights appeared in the road ahead and Carol veered towards them, throwing herself into the vehicle's path, oblivious to the danger. Wilbur Walsh, at the wheel, slammed on the brakes and narrowly missed hitting the young woman. Then, the woman startled Wilbur and his wife by running around the vehicle and scrambling into the back seat. "Drive!" she screamed. "Please drive."

Carol DaRonch was taken to the Murray Police Station where she made a tearful statement, describing how she'd been lured from the mall and then abducted. She held up the handcuffs still attached to her wrist as proof. The detective who took her statement assured her that there was no Officer Roseland working for the local force and that Murray police officers generally did not drive Bugs, not even as undercover vehicles. An APB had meanwhile been issued, instructing patrol cars to be on the lookout for the suspect VW.

Carol DaRonch had narrowly escaped death that night. But her good fortune would have tragic consequences for another young girl. Bundy was left angry and frustrated by Carol's escape. And he was still determined to find a victim.

Debby Kent

The city of Bountiful lies some 17 miles south of Murray in the shadow of the Wasatch Mountains. It is an area of outstanding natural beauty, a good place to raise children, a safe place to live. The Kent family, Dean, his wife Belva and their children Debby and Blair, certainly would not have wanted to live anywhere else.

On the night of November 8, while Carol DaRonch was making her desperate escape from Ted Bundy, the Kents were making plans for an evening out. Dean, Belva, and 17-year-old Debby were attending a production of "The Redhead" at Viewmont High School. Blair, who had no interest in the play, was going to the local roller rink, where his parents would pick him up later.

At around 8 o'clock that evening, Debby Kent was seated in the auditorium awaiting the curtain. Backstage, drama teacher Jean Graham was frantically directing final preparations when a stranger approached her. The young man politely asked if she would accompany him to the parking lot to identify a car but Jean said that she didn't have the time right now. He didn't press the issue.

About twenty minutes later, after the play had begun, Jean noticed the same man, still lurking in the shadows. He approached her again, smiling, his eyes never leaving hers. "Hey," he said. "Have you got some time to check out that car now? It will only take a minute."

Jean wasn't sure what it was about the man. He was well-dressed, well-groomed and exceedingly polite. Still, there was something about him that creeped her out. There was no way she was going anywhere with him. "I really can't," she said. "I'm in charge of the play. But if you like, I'll get my husband to give you a hand. If you'll wait right here, I'll go and call him." The man's expression seemed to change at that. The smile was gone in an instant. He turned and walked away without another word, leaving Jean perplexed as to who he was. Later, she'd spot him lurking around in the foyer.

By intermission, it was clear that the play was running late. Realizing that they were going to miss their arranged 10 p.m. pickup with Blair, Debby tried to phone her brother at the roller rink but couldn't get hold of him. She returned for the second act but agreed with her parents that she'd leave before the end, pick up Blair, and then return to collect them. She slipped out of the auditorium before the final curtain. And disappeared forever.

It did not take the Kents long to figure out that something was wrong. As the play concluded and the parking lot emptied they saw that their car was still parked where they'd left it. It appeared that Debby had never made it to the vehicle at all. So where was she? A search of the school grounds and buildings turned up no sign of the missing teenager and around midnight the police were called. They, of course, were well aware of the murder of Melissa Smith and the disappearance of Laura Aime so they responded quickly. Later, while questioning witnesses, they would learn of the stranger who had been seen lurking backstage and in the foyer, a man who closely matched the description that Carol DaRonch had given. If further proof were needed, they also found a handcuff key in the parking lot. They took the key back to the station, slotted it into the handcuffs that had been on Carol's wrist and gave it a twist. The cuffs opened.

Chapter 9: Without a Trace

During December 1974, a crime conference was held in Reno, Nevada, during which officers from various states presented unsolved cases in the hope that lawmen from other states and jurisdictions might have similar cases and that they could compare notes. Members of the King County task force were in attendance and did a presentation on their unsolved "Co-Ed Murders." Also at the conference were officers from Utah, who discussed the Smith, Aime, and Kent cases, as well as the attempted abduction of Carol DaRonch. But the connection was missed. Crimes against women are unfortunately an all too common occurrence in America.

The first time that Ted Bundy's name reached the ears of Utah investigators was when a somewhat hysterical Liz Kloepfer phoned it in. They noted it down but took no further action. Like their Washington colleagues, they were inundated with tip-offs and an honors graduate and law student did not seem like a promising suspect. Bundy, in any case, was playing it safe. The heat was on in Utah. He was now driving further afield in search of victims. As far as Colorado.

Caryn Campbell

Caryn Campbell was 23 years old and she was in love. The registered nurse was engaged to Dr. Raymond Gadowski, nine years her senior and the father of two children, Gregory, 11, and Jennifer, 9. She got on well with the kids and adored Raymond, even if he appeared to be stalling somewhat on their wedding plans.

In January 1975, Dr. Gadowski was invited to attend a Cardiology conference in Aspen, Colorado and decided to bring Caryn and the children along. He, of course, would be tied up most of the time in seminars but he figured it would be a great opportunity for Caryn to spend quality time with Greg and Jenny. They arrived from their Michigan base on January 11 and checked into the plush Wildwood Inn in Snowmass Village taking a suite on the second floor. Thereafter, Caryn and the kids did some sightseeing while Raymond hooked up with colleagues.

The following day, January 12, Dr. Gadowski attended the first of the lectures while Caryn and the children did some skiing. Caryn was nursing a slight flu that day but she did not allow that to distract from her enjoyment. That night, the group had dinner at a restaurant and then returned to the Wildwood. Not wanting to go up to their room yet, they settled down in the hotel's comfortable lounge. There, Greg picked up a newspaper while the youngsters occupied themselves by watching TV. Caryn, at a loose end, remembered that she had a magazine in her room and decided to go up and fetch it. On such small decisions do the wheels of fate turn.

All things considered, the round trip to the room and back should have taken Caryn Campbell no more than ten minutes. But ten minutes passed and then fifteen and then twenty. Raymond Gadowski began to get twitchy. What was keeping her? Eventually, he decided to go and check on Caryn. He knew that she was feeling a bit under the weather. Perhaps dinner hadn't agreed with her.

Since Caryn had the only key to the suite, Raymond rapped on the door and waited. He expected a quick response and when it didn't come, he knocked again, harder this time. Then he called out her name. Still nothing. Fearing now that something might have happened to Caryn, that she might have fainted and hit her head, he turned and sprinted down the corridor, down the stairs to the front desk. Minutes later, he was slotting a spare key into the door, twisting it and entering the suite. He half expected to find Caryn passed out on the floor but there was no sign of her in the room nor any indication that she'd ever been there.

Perplexed, Raymond left the room and walked back into the corridor. This being Saturday night and with a large conference in town, there were parties going on in several of the suites. Perhaps Caryn had been waylaid by someone she knew and dragged into one of the parties for a drink. Yes, that had to be it. But a quick tour of the events taking place on the floor produced no sign of Caryn, nor of anyone who had seen her. She wasn't in any of the hotel bars either and she hadn't somehow slipped by him and returned to the lounge. At around 10 p.m., Raymond Gadowski called the Aspen Police and reported his fiancée missing.

The police did not conduct a search that night but they did put out a bulletin on the missing woman. The following day, detectives converged on the Wildwood Inn and searched every room, every public space, every service area. They also questioned every guest at the hotel and drew a blank on that too. Somehow an attractive young woman had vanished from a busy hotel corridor and no one had seen or heard a thing.

Days passed without a word. Finally, Dr. Gadowski packed up his children and flew back to Michigan. He remained convinced that Caryn would phone him within a few days with a viable explanation for what had happened. He knew that she was keen to get married and was annoyed that he kept stalling on the issue. Perhaps this was her way of teaching him a lesson. If that was the case, he considered himself schooled.

But there was no word from Caryn and neither would there be. On February 18, six days after Caryn Campbell disappeared, a man was walking along Owl Creek Road, a few miles from the Wildwood Inn. His attention was arrested by a flight of squawking birds and when he went to investigate he spotted something half-buried in a snowbank, a sight that would remain with him for the rest of his life. Caryn Campbell had been brutally beaten to death and had also suffered numerous deep cuts to her body. A dislocated hyoid bone suggested that she had also been strangled. The corpse had been ravaged by animals making it impossible to determine whether she had been raped or not. However, the fact that she was found naked suggested that she had been.

So what had happened to Caryn Campbell? How had she disappeared from a busy, well-lit hotel corridor and ended up dead in a snowbank? Once again we must turn to Bundy's oblique confession to unravel the mystery.

If there's one thing we know about Ted Bundy it is that he was prepared to take huge risks in order to lure a victim. This behavior is, in fact, typical of the psychopath. He has a very low threshold for fear and is therefore always pushing the envelope in order to experience that addictive adrenalin rush. Psychopaths truly are oblivious to danger and Bundy certainly fits the bill. We have already seen the risks he took in snatching Georgann Hawkins and in luring Janice Ott and Denise Naslund from Lake Sammamish. As an exercise in outrageous risk-taking, the abduction of Caryn Campbell outdoes even those.

Bundy seems to have known that Caryn was a medical professional (or perhaps he guessed, since there was a large medical convention in town). And what better way to attract the attention of a doctor or nurse than to collapse at their feet feigning chest pains? Caryn, of course, had rushed to his aid and had been more than willing to assist when he'd asked if she would help him back to his room. (He'd booked in earlier using an assumed name and claiming that the room was for him and "his wife" in order to avert suspicion.) Bundy did not elaborate on where and how he killed Caryn but it must have been away from the hotel since the police carried out a search the next day and found nothing. More than likely, he strangled her into submission and then held her in his room, probably sexually assaulting her there. Then, after the parties died down, he'd snuck her out of the hotel and spirited her away into the night.

Chapter 10: Caught!

Six weeks after the discovery of Caryn Campbell's remains there was another gruesome find, this time in Washington State. On May 1, 1975, two Green River Community College students were hiking through the brush on Taylor Mountain when they found a human skull. Dental records would identify the victim as Brenda Ball, missing since May of the previous year. Cause of death was, of course, impossible to determine but the left side of the skull was caved in, indicating that she'd been bludgeoned. It also interested investigators that no other bones were found in the immediate vicinity. Even accounting for animal activity that is a most unlikely scenario. Was it possible that Brenda Ball had been decapitated?

In order to test that theory, and also to look for other remains, the police set up cordons and flooded the area with officers. And those efforts would soon be rewarded. On May 3, another skull was found bearing similar trauma to that of Brenda Ball. The victim would later be identified as Susan Rancourt. Fifty feet away, lay the skull of Roberta Kathleen Parks. And a short while later, officers found a fourth skull, this one belonging to the first victim, Lynda Ann Healy. Despite the search continuing for several days more, no other bones were found leaving detectives to draw the macabre conclusion that "Ted" had indeed decapitated his victims. To what purpose, they couldn't tell.

The King County suspect list which had begun at 2,247 names had now been whittled down to 200. Ted Bundy remained on the list but 200 is still an awful lot of suspects to process for a small police force and Bundy was far from the top of the pile. The police still believed that their perpetrator would have an arrest record for violence or sexual assault. Bundy had been picked up twice, for burglary and for car theft but he'd been a juvenile at the time and his record was sealed. Had the police been able to tie his departure from Washington to the sudden cessation of the murders there, they might have looked more closely at him but they had no way of making that connection. Bundy was now living in Utah and had already left his bloody imprint on the women of that state. Now he'd shifted his hunting ground again. With the murder of Caryn Campbell, his focus had transferred to Colorado.

Julie Cunningham

On the night of March 15, 26-year-old Julie Cunningham, a ski instructor from Vail, Colorado, had reason to feel down in the dumps. Her latest boyfriend had just ended their relationship and Julie was beginning to think that she was never going to find Mr. Right. Seeking to cheer her up, a friend had invited her to a local tavern for a few beers and Julie had reluctantly agreed. She left her apartment at around eight that evening and was never seen again. Her fate would remain a mystery until Ted Bundy admitted to her murder years later.

Bundy was out hunting again in early April, this time in Grand Junction, Colorado, just over the border with Utah. Twenty-five-year-old Denise Oliverson had argued with her husband on the Sunday afternoon of April 6, and had stormed off on her bicycle, headed for her parents' home a few miles away. She never made it. All that was ever found of her was her bike and her sandals, left abandoned under a bridge on US 50.

Denise Oliverson

There were other murdered girls, too. Twelve-year-old Lynette Culver was abducted from Alameda Junior High School in Pocatello, Idaho on May 6, 1975. Susan Curtis, 15, disappeared during a youth conference at Brigham Young University in Provo Utah on June 28, 1975. Neither girl's body has ever been found. Eighteen-year-old Melanie Cooley went missing from the tiny town of Nederland on April 15 and was found eight days later, raped, bludgeoned and strangled. Shelly Kay Robinson failed to show up for work in Golden, Colorado on July 1. Her brutalized body was found in a mineshaft at the foot of Berthold Pass on August 21. The corpse bore all the hallmarks of a Bundy victim. There may well have been other victims. If there were, their deaths went unreported or were not connected to the rampaging killer.

But Ted Bundy's career as a free-ranging serial killer was about to be brought to an abrupt, if temporary, end. In the early hours of Friday, August 15, 1975, Utah Highway Patrol Sergeant Bob Hayward, pulled to a stop outside his home in Granger, Utah. Hayward was not on duty at the time but the 22-year veteran of the force was no less vigilant for it and when a light-colored VW Bug went drifting past he was immediately alert. He knew everyone in the neighborhood and none of them drove a Bug. What was the car doing here then, at 2:30 in the morning? Hayward decided to find out. Pulling away from the curb, he set off in pursuit of the VW, switching on his brights so that he could get a look at the license plate. The minute he did so, the Bug's lights were turned off and the car raced away into the night.

Hayward gave chase, following the Bug as it sped through two stop signs without slowing. But there was only going to be one winner in this particular race and the driver of the VW must have realized that. He pulled over eventually at a gas station. Hayward then got out of his car and approached the suspect vehicle. The man behind the wheel looked about twenty-five years old with wild, longish hair. Hayward asked for his driver's license and the man handed it over. It identified him as Theodore Robert Bundy.

"You do realize that you ran two stop signs back there, right?" Hayward said.

"I guess I'm lost," Bundy said with a sheepish grin. He then went on to explain that he'd been to a showing of 'The Towering Inferno' at a nearby drive-in.

If that was meant to allay the officer's suspicions, it had the opposite effect. Hayward knew that that movie was not currently showing. He peered into the car with renewed interest and saw that the passenger seat had been removed. He also spotted a small crowbar lying on the floor behind the driver's seat.

"Mind if I look inside the car?" Hayward asked.

At this point, both men were distracted by the splash of headlights. A police cruiser had pulled in behind them, although the two officers remained in the vehicle.

"Do you mind if I look inside your car?" Hayward repeated.

"Er... sure," Bundy said, popping the door and stepping out. Hayward then began his search and immediately spotted a gym bag in the passenger footwell. Inside he found another crowbar, a ski mask, rope, handcuffs, wire and an ice pick. Hayward knew exactly what it was – a burglary kit. He therefore placed Bundy under arrest, charging him with reckless driving and attempting to evade a law officer.

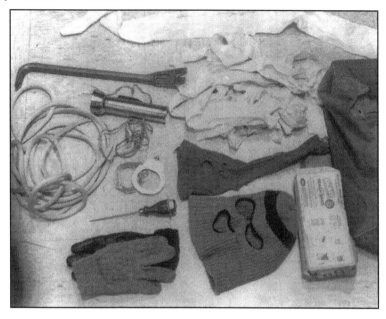

"Burglary kit" found in Bundy's car

Bundy was taken to a local police station where a thorough search of his bag turned up more suspicious items – a flashlight, gloves, strips of torn sheeting, handcuffs and a mask made from a pair of pantyhose. These items were retained as evidence, with police officers informing Bundy that the D.A. was likely to bring charges for possession of burglary tools. Bundy seemed unconcerned by that prospect.

On August 18, Salt Lake City Detective Jerry Thompson was going over the weekend's arrest records when one name caught his eye – Bundy. Where had he recently heard that name? Thompson was, of course, the lead investigator in the Melissa Smith murder inquiry and it eventually dawned on him. The woman who had phoned from Seattle tipping the Utah Police off to her boyfriend. It

hadn't seemed like a promising lead at the time but now
Thompson's interest was roused.

Pulling Bundy's arrest sheet, Thompson saw that he'd been driving
a tan VW Bug. Wasn't that the same type of vehicle used in the
attempted abduction of that girl in Murray? He pulled the DaRonch
file and saw that it was. And there was another interesting piece of
information. The handcuffs that had been left dangling from Carol
DaRonch's wrist had been an unusual foreign brand, Jana. The
cuffs that had been found in Bundy's bag were of a different make,
Gerocal, but Thompson couldn't help but wonder how many young
men drove around with handcuffs in their possession. And of
course, handcuffs had also played a role in the Debby Kent
abduction. The police had found a handcuff key at the scene.
Thompson felt a sudden rush of exhilaration, the kind
investigators experience when the pieces of a puzzle begin to slot
together.

On August 21, Bundy was arrested for being in possession of
burglary tools, a misdemeanor and one that he fully expected to
beat. He had already crafted innocent explanations for all of the
items found in his vehicle and he was also now insisting that he'd
never given Sergeant Hayward permission to search the car. That,
of course, would have seen the charges against him thrown out.
But what Bundy didn't know was that there was a flurry of police
work going on behind the scenes, work that would see him facing
far more serious charges. Detective Thompson was by now
convinced that Bundy was the man who had tried to abduct Carol
DaRonch and had succeeded in snatching Melissa Smith, Laura
Aime and Debby Kent.

A search of Bundy's apartment might provide supporting evidence and Bundy willingly signed a consent-to-search form and then stood smirking in the background while detectives went through his stuff. They found nothing of use to their investigation although they did find some items that would soon be of interest to their colleagues across the state line – a map of Colorado with several locations, including the Wildwood Inn, marked. Before he departed, Thompson asked Bundy whether he could take some pictures of his VW Bug and Bundy willingly agreed. It would be the last time Bundy was so cooperative with the police. Thereafter, he acquired a lawyer and clammed up.

On September 16, 1975, Detectives Jerry Thompson, Dennis Crouch and Ira Beal, flew from Salt Lake City to Seattle to question Elizabeth Kloepfer. It was Liz's tip-off that had steered them in the direction of Ted Bundy in the first place, but she had paid a heavy price for it. Liz still loved Ted and despite everything she still wanted to believe in his innocence. As she walked into the interview room at the King County Police Major Crime Unit building in Seattle, it was clear that she was under heavy emotional stress. She immediately lit up a cigarette and would not be without one during the long interview, burning her way through the full pack.

Still, the information that Liz provided served only to fortify the investigators' belief that Ted Bundy was a mass murderer. She told the officers that Bundy often went out in the middle of the night, destination unknown. He kept odd items in his car, like an oriental knife and a lug wrench with a taped handle, he had crutches and

Plaster of Paris in his room for which he could provide no explanation. Most pertinently, his presence was unaccounted for on every night that a girl went missing. Liz had checked the dates against a calendar and was certain of that. She went on to say that Bundy's sexual behavior had changed over the past year (during the timespan that the Washington murders had occurred). Previously he'd been a gentle lover but now he was only interested in bondage and anal sex. On one occasion, he'd put his hands on her throat and had throttled her to the point where she had almost passed out.

All of this was very interesting, of course, but it was circumstantial. The Utah investigators were covering ground that had already been well furrowed by their Washington counterparts. They too had been left frustrated. There were dozens of intersections, multiple snippets of information that tied Bundy to the missing and murdered girls. Bundy was a close fit for eyewitness descriptions; he'd driven a bronze-colored Bug in Washington and now drove a tan one in Utah. Credit card receipts placed him in many of the towns where murders had occurred; the first attacks had occurred within walking distance of his residence; he'd been spotted at Lake Sammamish in the week prior to the Ott and Naslund murders; he had crutches and Plaster of Paris in his room – both had been used as props in the murders; a friend had seen him with his arm in a cast even though there was no record that he had ever suffered a fracture.

It all made for a compelling circumstantial case but not one that any D.A. worth his salt was going to bring before the courts.

And it seemed for a time as though the DaRonch case was heading down a similar path. Carol DaRonch and Jean Graham, the Viewmont High drama teacher, were shown a photo array and asked to identify the man they'd seen. The teacher pointed out Bundy immediately but DaRonch wavered and said that she thought Bundy was the man but couldn't be sure. And she was even less certain when shown a picture of Bundy's VW.

Bundy's VW Bug on display at the National Crime Museum

It was a blow to the investigation but not a fatal one. The police still had the option of putting Bundy into a lineup. That process took place on October 2, 1975, with three witnesses – Carol DaRonch, Jean Graham, and Jolynne Beck, a friend of Debby Kent who had encountered a stranger in the auditorium on the night Debby disappeared. All three women immediately picked out Ted Bundy. Thereafter, Bundy was arrested and charged with attempted kidnapping and aggravated assault. Unable to make bail, he was sent to the County lockup to await trial.

Chapter 11: Escape from Colorado

Ted Bundy's kidnapping trial eventually got underway in Salt Lake City on Monday, February 23, 1976, before Judge Stewart Hanson. In the interim, Bundy had been out on bond, his $15,000 bail raised by friends and family. He had remained under constant surveillance during that time, both in Salt Lake City and during a trip back to Seattle.

Bundy was supremely confident of walking on the charges. So much so, in fact, that he waived his right to a jury trial and left the decision as to his guilt or innocence in the hands of Judge Hanson, a man with a reputation for treating defendants fairly. And, at first, Bundy's confidence seemed vindicated. Carol DaRonch did not come across as the most reliable of witnesses. She broke down and sobbed several times as she described the events of sixteen months earlier. And she buckled under cross-examination by Bundy's attorney, tearfully refuting his suggestion that the cops had browbeaten her into identifying Bundy as the man who had attacked her. Asked to point out that man she directed an accusing finger at Ted Bundy.

But the man she was indicating looked anything but a criminal. He was smartly attired in a gray suit, white shirt and tie, and he was clean-shaven, his hair neatly trimmed. He was also extremely articulate, taking the stand in his own defense to explain away the evidence against him. Had the case been tried before a jury, it is highly likely that he would have walked.

But the decision was left to Judge Hanson and, on Monday, March
1, 1976, he found Bundy guilty of aggravated kidnapping and
remanded him to the custody of the Salt Lake County Sherriff's
office to await sentencing. That sentence was eventually handed
down on June 1. Fifteen years behind bars was a harsh term for a
first time offender but in truth, Ted Bundy had got off lightly. He'd
been charged only for the least of his misdeeds.

What Bundy didn't realize was that his legal problems were about
to escalate. While he'd been awaiting trial, forensics teams had
torn his VW apart, going over it with a fine-toothed comb in the
hunt for evidence. Bundy, like most psychopaths, had always been
convinced that he was smarter than the police. He had gone to
extraordinary lengths to avoid leaving trace evidence behind at his
crime scenes and fully believed that they had nothing on him. But
such an undertaking is nigh on impossible. The VW yielded two
hairs, which were sent to the FBI Crime Lab for analysis. They
were found to be similar to hairs from Caryn Campbell and Melissa
Smith. Additionally, the crowbar found in Bundy's car produced a
perfect match to the distinctive injuries inflicted on Caryn
Campbell's skull. On October 22, 1976, the state of Colorado filed
charges against Bundy for murder. In January 1977, they obtained
an extradition order.

The many faces of Ted Bundy

Bundy was transferred to the Pitkin County Jail in Aspen, Colorado where he promptly fired his court-appointed attorneys and declared that he would be conducting his own defense. That, of course, entitled him to certain privileges, like access to a law library and unlimited phone calls. He used these to the max, even calling investigators in Seattle in a bid to gain information that he said was vital to his defense. They offered to provide it on a quid pro quo basis. Bundy declined.

In the meantime, moves were afoot to transfer Bundy to a new home. The Colorado Health Department had ruled that Pitkin was a short-term facility and that no inmate could be held there for longer than thirty days. The result was that Bundy was sent to

Garfield County Jail in Glenwood Springs. Not that Ted minded, it meant that deputies had to drive him to Aspen several times a week so that he could visit the courthouse library. Those trips took 45 minutes each way and Bundy was in cuffs and leg irons for the duration.

On June 7, 1977, Bundy was again brought along that familiar route. This time, however, it was for a hearing, a hearing to determine whether the death penalty would be a consideration in his case. At the courthouse, Bundy was placed in the custody of Deputy David Westerlund, an officer who had guarded him on only one previous occasion.

Proceedings began promptly at 9 a.m. with a public defender delivering a vociferous argument against capital punishment. That argument concluded at 10:30 when the judge called a recess. Bundy, as he usually did, retired to the library for the break, and soon lost himself in the stacks. His guard, Westerlund, stationed himself at the door, the only exit from the room. Bundy was not continually in Westerlund's line of sight but that didn't concern the officer too much. The library was on the second floor, a twenty-five foot drop to the paving stones below.

But the deputy had underestimated his prisoner's desperate desire to be free. At around 10:40, a woman passing by the court building saw a man hanging from the sill of a second floor window. Then the man loosened his grip and dropped to the ground, landing awkwardly. As the woman watched, he scurried to his feet and then set off down the road, limping badly on one leg. Not really sure what she'd just witnessed, the woman decided to report the incident. Then, a quick search of the library uncovered the frightening truth. Ted Bundy, suspected serial killer, was on the run.

The news sent the entire Aspen police force scampering. Road blocks were hurriedly set up, tracking dogs were called in and officers on horseback were sent into the surrounding countryside. They fully expected to make a quick capture. Bundy, after all, was on foot and he was apparently injured. Even though his cuffs and leg irons had been removed for the court appearance, he couldn't get far. All of the roads heading out of town had been cut off and the only other escape route was through the mountains. No one but a fool would attempt that. No one but a fool or Ted Bundy.

Bundy had indeed headed into the foothills. His plan was to lay low, let the search take its course and eventually die down. Then, once his pursuers had begun to believe that he'd eluded them, once the roadblocks were dismantled, he'd head back into town, steal a car and drive right out of there.

It was an audacious plan, one that required everything to go his way. Over the next week, Bundy managed to lay low, subsisting on food stolen from the holiday cabins that dotted the Aspen hills. Meanwhile, a massive search continued, the posse getting so close that Ted could hear the baying of the hounds. Eventually, though, it was the cold and hunger that got to him rather than the searchers. The food he'd managed to steal was barely enough to keep him alive let alone fuel his escape; his sprained ankle throbbed constantly and kept him awake at night; the clothes he was wearing were ill-suited to the nighttime temperatures, even in summer. He was exhausted, cold and hungry. If there was a play to be made, he had to make it now, while he still had the strength.

And so, Ted Bundy headed back into town and there he was spotted and taken into custody. His bid for freedom had lasted six days and gained him nothing but the increased vigilance of his jailers. From now on, he would be required to wear leg irons and handcuffs at all times, other than when he was in the courtroom conducting his defense.

The months that followed were punctuated by court appearances and legal maneuvering by both teams. First the prosecution filed a motion to have details of the Utah murders entered into evidence. This was refused by the judge, much to Bundy's delight. Then Bundy filed a motion for a change of venue which the judge approved, moving the proceedings to Colorado Springs, 60 miles south of Aspen. In the midst of all this, Bundy got word from Utah that his appeal in the DaRonch case had been turned down.

There was better news on December 27. The judge had handed down his ruling regarding sentencing in the Campbell trial. The death penalty was off the table. Not that it would make a whole lot of difference. Ted Bundy would never stand trial for the murder of Caryn Campbell. He was about to make another bid for freedom. And this time, he would succeed.

During the Christmas holidays, the Garfield County Jail was a deserted place. All of the short term prisoners had been sent home to spend the festive period with their families. Bundy, in fact, was the only inmate in the entire facility. Most of the guards and support staff had been granted leave too. Only Bob Morrison of the four regular jailers remained on duty.

Ted Bundy, who seldom did anything without a plan, had been waiting on this moment. Over the prior months he'd accumulated a lot of information about the prison. He'd studied the movements of the guards and learned the layout of the place from a cellmate. More importantly, he'd acquired a hacksaw, carried in for him by someone from the outside whose identity he would never reveal. Bundy had also uncovered a weakness in the structure of his cell. There was a metal plate fixed to the ceiling where a light fitting was to be installed. Budgetary cuts had delayed the installation of that fitting and given Bundy a unique window of opportunity. Over the prior eight weeks he'd meticulously cut a hole, twelve-by-twelve inches, into the metal, working so carefully that the cut was invisible to cursory inspection. He'd timed his labors to coincide with shower time, when the drumming of water and the shouts of the inmates drowned out the sound of the blade biting into metal.

Twelve-by-twelve is a very small hole for a man to wiggle through, especially a tall man like Bundy. But he'd accounted for that. Over the previous few months, he'd cut down on his calorie intake and had dropped a considerable amount of weight. Was it enough to allow him to squeeze through the small gap? Bundy had tested that in the nights leading up to his escape and found that it was.

His escape hatch had delivered him into a tight cinderblock shaft. Crawling along it, he'd come to a place where the concrete below him became wood. A slim shaft of light penetrated a gap to the side of the wood panel and Bundy heard voices from beyond it. Getting a grip on the panel he'd shifted it ever so slightly and peered through. He'd found himself looking down into the interior of a closet in one of the jailers' apartments. Replacing the panel, he'd backed up along the shaft and then dropped back into his cell. He had his way out. All he had to do now was wait for the right moment. That moment came on the night of December 30.

Bundy waited until all was quiet within the prison and then quickly removed the metal plate above his head. He pulled himself into the dusty shaft and then inched his way along the concrete until he reached the wooden panel. Lift it and he could drop into the closet, change into civilian clothes and then walk from the apartment directly out onto the street.

But this path was fraught with danger. If he chose the wrong closet and ended up in the apartment of Bob Morrison, the only jailer on duty, or if he encountered Morrison on his way out, he was dead, whether literally or figuratively. Either option was better, he decided, than sitting in a cell waiting for a trial that would likely deliver him to a life sentence.

But luck was with Bundy this night, as it often was. The apartment that he chose was empty. After easing himself into the closet, he changed his prison uniform for jeans and a turtleneck sweater. Then he simply walked to freedom.

Bundy had made one other preparation during the months leading up to his escape. He'd stopped eating breakfast, leaving his food untouched outside his cell. So when his morning meal again went uneaten on December 31, his jailer peeped through the keyhole, saw a form under the blankets and assumed that Ted was still asleep. It was lunchtime before the guard entered the cell, pulled the covers back and found the pile of legal papers that his prisoner had stacked there. By then, Ted Bundy was in downtown Chicago.

After walking away from the prison, Bundy had stolen an MG Midget, which he'd driven out of Glenwood Springs into a gathering gale. The car's engine had blown on the pass out of town but Bundy had quickly thumbed a ride to Vail. From there he'd taken a bus to Denver, arriving at around 8:30. Then it was a short cab ride to the airport. As his breakfast stood cooling outside his cell in Colorado, Bundy was on a flight to Illinois. On January 6, while the furor over his escape raged on, he was driving a stolen car out of Ann Arbor, Michigan, headed south. In Atlanta, he abandoned the vehicle and boarded a Trailways bus for Tallahassee, Florida. Ted Bundy had always had a thing for university towns.

Chapter 12: The Chi Omega Murders

By the time Ted Bundy stepped off the bus in Tallahassee on Sunday, January 8, 1978, he had determined upon one thing. Florida was going to be different. Here, he'd blend into the background, get a job, keep his nose clean. He wouldn't so much as attract a jaywalking ticket. Over the past week, while making his circuitous journey south, he'd undergone one of those physical transformations that came so naturally to him. He'd cultivated a beard to go with the hair that now curled around his ears and touched his collar. He also had a new identity. He was Chris Hagen now, not Ted Bundy.

Tallahassee, as it turned out, was the perfect place for him to blend in. And he'd timed his arrival perfectly. In that first week of January, nearly 30,000 students had streamed into the city, ready to begin the new semester at Florida State University. Bundy walked among them with the sun baking down out of a clear blue sky and he felt at peace. Freedom, after so many months behind bars was like an elixir. He felt totally at home among the beautiful people who milled around him.

The first order of business was a place to stay and he found one in a dilapidated rooming house called 'The Oak' on West College Avenue close to the FSU campus. The rent was $160 per month with a $100 security deposit. Since Bundy only had $160 left from his 'traveling money' he had to employ all of his charm to convince the landlord to give him the room. He paid the deposit and promised to pony up two months' rent within the next few weeks. That, of course, put pressure on him to find a job, and quick.

But Bundy did not exactly exert himself in his hunt for gainful employment. Over the days that followed, he fell into a routine of eating breakfast at the university's canteen, wandering the campus during the day, and eating dinner at fast food restaurants. He spent the evenings in his room, drinking beer and watching TV, chastising himself for his lethargy and promising that tomorrow he'd put a more concerted effort into finding a job. Within days he'd broken another of the promises he'd made to himself. He'd stolen a bicycle from a nearby residence. That threshold crossed, he began stealing other items, a TV set, some racquetball equipment, a plant for his room. From there it was just a short hop before he began lifting wallets and stealing cars. Ted Bundy's firm resolve to go straight had lasted just two days. His abstinence from murder would endure for only a few days longer.

Lisa Levy (left) and Margaret Bowman

The Chi Omega house stood on West Jefferson Street, a stone's throw from the FSU campus and a short walk from the boarding house where Ted Bundy now lived. It was home to thirty-nine beautiful and talented young women, a safe haven where entrance was via a combination lock to which only the students and their house mother had the code. To a predator like Ted Bundy, it hardly qualified as a barrier.

Bundy had walked past the house on his first day in Tallahassee, noticed all of the pretty women hanging around and deliberately averted his eyes and stepped up his pace. No point pushing temptation into the path of his new, reformed self. But that 'reformed self' had not endured for long and the next time that Bundy visited the Chi Omega house it was to engage in one of his favorite pastimes. He wanted to peek into the windows, to get a look at the women inside. Bundy was basically following the path that had led him to murder in the first place, graduating from theft to peeping and then... then the old urges were stirred up inside of him, bubbling near the surface. On the night of January 14, he gave in to them.

That Saturday night, the first of the new term, was a big one on campus, with several parties in progress. The popular student hangout, Sherrod's (which was located right next door to the Chi Omega house) was also doing a roaring trade.

Several of the Chi Omega women, including Lisa Levy, Melanie Nelson and Leslie Waddell, were at Sherrod's that night. So too, was a tall and gangly young man, who spooked another student, when he asked her to dance. Mary Ann Piccano would later tell police that the man did nothing overt but that he'd stared so intensely at her that he gave her the creeps. By the time the dance ended and she walked back to her seat, she was trembling uncontrollably. When she looked up again, the man was gone.

At around 2 a.m., Melanie Nelson and Leslie Waddell left Sherrod's and walked next door to their sorority house. When they reached the back door, they found it standing ajar, something that bothered Melanie but that Leslie shrugged off. Over the previous few days they'd been having a problem with the door. More than likely one of their sorority sisters had entered early and had failed to pull it hard enough to engage the lock. The girls entered the house and retired to bed.

About an hour later, another of the house's residents, Nita Neary was dropped off by her boyfriend. Nita had attended one of the many beer parties on campus that night but she was nursing a cold and hadn't had much to drink. She too found the door standing ajar but like Leslie she was not alarmed. That is, until she stepped into the downstairs rec room and heard a loud thump from above, followed by the sound of someone running. The footfalls appeared to be coming down the front staircase and so frightened Nita that she shrunk back into the shadows. That was when she saw him, a tall, slim man dressed in dark clothing and wearing a navy blue watch cap pulled over the top half of his face but leaving his nose exposed. The man was crouched over, almost gargoyle like, that impression strengthen by what he held in his hand, a wooden log that he gripped like a club.

Nita pressed back against the wall, too frightened even to breathe. She felt certain that if the man spotted her, she was dead. A second passed, one that felt like an hour. Then the man was twisting the door handle, throwing the door open and disappearing into the night. Still uncertain of what she'd just witnessed, Nita ran upstairs to wake her roommate, Nancy Dowdy.

"There's a man in the house," she hissed to the startled Nancy.

"What?" Nancy said, still bleary-eyed from sleep.

"There's a man in the house," Nita repeated. "I think we've been burgled."

Eventually, the girls plucked up the courage to check it out. They descended the stairs holding on to one another, Nancy clutching an umbrella by way of protection. There, they found the back door open and pulled it shut. Other than that, everything else appeared normal. They walked back up to the second floor convinced that Nita had overreacted. Perhaps it had all been an innocent misunderstanding. Perhaps one of the girls had smuggled a man into her room. They had almost begun to believe that when the door to number 8 swung open and one of their sorority sisters, Karen Chandler staggered out into the passage ahead of them. Karen was moaning, her hands held to her head. For a moment, they thought that she might be ill. Then they noticed the blood.

While Nancy tried to comfort the stricken girl, Nita ran to fetch the housemother, Mom Crenshaw. Then they entered Room 8 and found Kathy Kleiner, Karen's roommate sitting on the bed, moaning in a low almost animalistic expression of pain. She too was covered in blood.

A frantic 911 call now brought police and paramedics racing to the Chi Omega house, with the first units arriving minutes later at 3:23. While officers questioned Nita about the man she'd seen, and then broadcast a description to patrol units in the area, medics got to work on the battered girls. Both had suffered horrendous injuries. Karen Chandler had multiple abrasions to her face, a broken jaw, broken teeth and possible fractures to her skull. Kathy Kleiner had similar injuries and was also bleeding profusely from the mouth. The room in which they'd been attacked, resembled a slaughterhouse, with sprays of blood covering the walls, the drapes and the furniture. As neither girl had defensive wounds, and neither had cried out, it was assumed that they had been struck as they slept.

And yet, Karen and Kathy were the lucky ones. They had survived. As officers continued their search of the house, they entered Room 2 and found Lisa Levy lying on her bed. Lisa had not been beaten. Her pallid complexion, the blue tinge of her lips and the swelling around her throat pointed to strangulation. But the killer hadn't stopped there. He'd savaged her body with his teeth, almost biting off one of her nipples. There were bite marks on her buttocks too and the killer had inflicted another indignity. He'd raped and sodomized his victim with an aerosol can.

The paramedics knew instinctively that there was nothing that could be done for Lisa but still they tried, to get a pulse going, to force some breath into her lungs, to coax back any spark of life that still might flicker. It was all in vain. Lisa Levy was dead.

So, too, was Margaret Bowman in Room 9. She had suffered the most savage beating of all, the blows delivered with such ferocity that they had cracked open her skull and left her brain exposed. Not content, the killer had pulled a nylon stocking around Margaret's throat, cinching it so tightly that he'd cut into flesh. Margaret had not been sexually assaulted. By then, the attacker was in a murderous fury and had gone in search of new victims, finding Karen Chandler and Kathy Kleiner.

A reconstruction of events would later determine that they killer had been inside the house a mere fifteen minutes. Fifteen minutes! What kind of a monster, the first responders wondered, could wreak such wanton destruction in a mere fifteen minutes? The authorities in Washington, in Utah, and in Colorado could have told them. A monster named Ted Bundy. And Bundy's night of terror wasn't over yet.

After fleeing the Chi Omega house, he'd traveled eight blocks, to an old duplex on Dunwoody Street. Three young female students lived here, Debbie Ciccarelli and Nancy Young in one apartment, Cheryl Thomas in the other. At around 4 a.m., Debbie was awakened by a loud thumping noise that appeared to be coming from the apartment next door. The sounds continued for about ten seconds and then abruptly stopped, leaving Debbie so afraid that she woke her roommate. The two of them then lay fearfully in the dark, trying to discern what the sound had been and hoping that there was some innocent explanation for it. Then they heard a new sound, one that terrified them even more, the keening wail of someone who was obviously in pain. Afraid to go next door and check it out, the girls dialed their neighbor's number and heard it ring several times without being answered. Their next call was to the police. Within minutes, half-a-dozen patrol cars had screeched to a halt outside the building.

Cheryl Thomas was found lying diagonally across her bed in a pool of blood. She was semi-conscious, whimpering in pain but otherwise unresponsive. Her face was severely swollen, already turning an ugly shade of purple and it was clear that she had suffered serious head injuries. She was rushed to Tallahassee Memorial Hospital where ER doctors would spend the next hours fighting desperately to save her life. Thanks to their efforts, Cheryl would survive, although the attack would leave her with impaired hearing and balance problems. She'd been a promising ballerina with dreams of a career as a dancer. Those dreams were now gone forever.

The vicious attacks at the Chi Omega house and at Dunwoody Street had left the university town reeling. The atrocities also left the police extremely concerned. A man who could commit such acts of savagery was very likely to reoffend. Patrols were thus doubled around the university district and officers were placed at strategic locations, some in marked cars, others undercover. Not that any of these measures seemed to give much peace of mind to the student population. By night the streets were all but deserted.

No effort was spared in the hunt for the killer. The police had initially been confident that he must have left behind some clue to his identity, a fingerprint perhaps or a shoe print left in the blood of his victims. After all, he could hardly have been acting rationally in the midst of such carnage.

Except, it seemed that he had. There was plenty of evidence but not a single workable clue, save for Nita Neary's sighting of the killer and the bite marks he'd inflicted on Lisa Levy. Neither of those was worth much until they had a suspect in custody.

So where was their suspect? After the attack on Cheryl Thomas, Bundy had returned to his boarding house. In the early hours of Sunday morning, two other tenants had spotted him standing on the porch looking out into the dark even as the sound of sirens filled the night air. The following day, the same two men, Henry Polumbo and Rus Gage, had been discussing the murders when Bundy joined in the conversation and offered his opinion. "This was a professional job," he'd said. "The guy who did this has done it before. He's probably long gone by now."

Chapter 13: Little Girl Gone

Why Bundy chose to stay in Tallahassee after the Chi Omega murders is a mystery. The police presence in the area was overbearing and there was mention in the press that an eyewitness had seen the attacker. Bundy didn't see how that was possible but what if it was? As someone who fit the general description, he might be pulled in for questioning at any time and if the police ran a background check they would soon discover that he wasn't Chris Hagen but a fugitive from justice, wanted in connection with several murders out west.

So the sensible course of action would have been to get out of Tallahassee while the getting was good. Except, Bundy didn't do that. Instead, he hung around and even continued his campaign of purse-snatching and car theft. Before long, he'd begun to think about going hunting again.

On the afternoon of Wednesday, February 8, 1978, 14-year-old Leslie Parmenter was standing outside Jeb Stuart Junior High in Jacksonville, Florida. Leslie was the daughter of Jacksonville PD's Chief of Detectives, James Parmenter, and she was waiting for her brother Danny. Only Danny was late and, growing impatient, Leslie decided to cross the road to wait in the K-Mart parking lot. At least that way, Danny wouldn't have to make a U-turn when he eventually got here.

It was raining that day in Jacksonville and as Leslie bowed her head against the increasing drizzle, a white Dodge van suddenly raced across the lot, screeching to a halt just a few feet from her. A young man sprang from the driver's seat and approached purposefully. The badge pinned to his navy blue jacket read: "Richard Burton, Fire Department." Only he didn't look like a fire official. He had wild, tousled hair and a few days' worth of stubble on his chin.

"Do you attend the school over there?" the man asked. "Are you going to the K-Mart?"

Leslie looked at the man perplexed. What did it have to do with the fire department what school she attended? Also, she didn't like the way the man was looking at her. He gave her the creeps. She tried to sidestep the man but he stepped in front of her, cutting off her escape. She had the distinct impression that he was trying to channel her towards his van. It was at that moment that Danny Parmenter rolled into the lot.

Danny noticed immediately the white van cutting off Leslie's escape, the scruffy-looking man talking to her, the look of terror on his sister's face. He pulled up beside the stranger and demanded to know what he wanted. "Nothing," the man mumbled, but Danny was not about to let him off the hook that easy. Instructing Leslie to get into his truck, he got out and confronted the stranger.

"What did you want with my sister?" he demanded.

"Nothing," the man said, backing away. "I thought she was someone else." Then he scrambled into his van and raced out of the lot. But not before Danny Parmenter noted down his license plate number, 13-D-11300.

Leslie Parmeter did not know it at the time but she had just survived an encounter with America's most notorious serial killer. Her escape would spell doom for another little girl.

Kimberly Leach

Kimberley Leach was a pretty, dark-haired 12-year-old who attended Lake City Junior High in Lake City, Florida, roughly halfway between Jacksonville and Tallahassee. On the morning of February 9, 1978, Kimberley was on her way to a gym class when she realized that she'd left her purse behind in her home room.

Going back to retrieve it meant exiting one school building, walking out onto the street and entering another building. Kimberley made this short journey in the company of a friend, Priscilla Blakney, but Priscilla loitered a while longer in the home room and Kim left a few seconds ahead of her. When Priscilla went running after her friend, she saw Kimberley being beckoned towards a white van by a stranger.

Clinch Enfield, a school crossing guard, also saw the van. So too did Clarence Anderson, an off-duty paramedic who was annoyed that the vehicle was blocking traffic. Anderson would later testify that he saw a young, dark-haired girl being led towards the van by a man in a dark jacket and aviator glasses. The man had a beard and untidy hair and he appeared to be angry at something. Anderson assumed that he was an irate parent, called to pick his daughter up from school because of some misdemeanor. The girl appeared to be in tears.

For some reason, Priscilla Blakney had made no mention to her teachers of Kimberley walking towards the white van. Perhaps she was afraid of getting her friend into trouble. It was only later that afternoon that Kimberley's absence was noted. Then, a school employee phoned Kim's mother to inquire about her whereabouts. Freda Leach was startled by the call. She had assumed that her daughter was in school. When the school administrator suggested that Kimberley might have run away, Freda was adamant that her daughter would never do such a thing. Kim was a diligent student and an obedient child. Besides, she had been so excited by the upcoming Valentine's Ball for which she had been elected as a princess. There was no way on earth that she would have wanted to miss that.

The Leaches might have been adamant that Kimberley hadn't run away but they at least entertained the possibility that their daughter might have veered from her usually dependable path and played hooky from the last few periods of school. Perhaps they even hoped that was the case. But as the afternoon headed towards evening, as their calls to Kimberley's friends produced no indication of her whereabouts, they began to become more and more concerned. Then they spoke to Priscilla and heard the story of the stranger in the white van. Their next call was to the police.

A bulletin was issued to all patrol cars that night, advising them to be on the lookout for a dark-haired twelve-year-old, five-foot tall and weighing about 100 pounds, possibly in the company of an adult male driving a white van.

The Lake City police were not the only one's looking for that van. After the attempted abduction of Leslie Parmenter the previous day, Leslie's brother Danny had written down the license number of the van the suspected kidnapper had been driving. That information was passed on to his father James, Jacksonville's Chief of Detectives. Checks had determined that the plates had been stolen from a vehicle parked on Dunwoody Street in Tallahassee. That street was, of course, where Cheryl Thomas had been so brutally attacked and James Parmenter wondered if there might be a link. Then he heard the report of the girl missing from Lake City, and Parmenter felt a ripple of gooseflesh up his arms. He was suddenly certain that all of these cases were connected, suddenly convinced that his daughter had come within seconds of certain death.

A massive search was launched for Kimberley Leach, one that would endure for eight weeks before its tragic denouement. Ted Bundy, meanwhile, was back in Tallahassee and he was slowly coming apart. Gone was the smooth, suave, impeccably groomed Ted who could so easily dupe pretty girls into perilous situations. Now his hair was long and his beard was scruffy and he was reduced to using force rather than guile to lure his victims. He was also becoming paranoid. On every corner, he saw police cruisers and he was convinced that they were all watching him. Quite aside from that, he owed his landlord $320, a payment that was due imminently and one which he had no means of servicing. The walls felt as though they were closing in on him and placed in that situation, he did the only thing he could. He fled.

Chapter 14: America's Most Wanted

On the evening of February 12, Bundy spent a few hours wiping down his room at the Oaks. He'd already done the same with the white Dodge van he'd been using. That vehicle stood abandoned several blocks away. He now had another ride, an orange VW Bug which he'd found on a side street with the keys dangling from the ignition. Bundy had always been partial to Bugs. Later that night, while the rest of the household was asleep, he carried his meager possessions down to the VW and then drove out of town, headed west. The following day, he was in Crestview, some 150 miles away, where he got into an argument with a hotel clerk who refused his stolen credit card. Then he dropped off the radar, reappearing in Pensacola, Florida in the early morning hours of Tuesday, February 15.

Officer David Lee, a patrolman working for the Pensacola PD, was sitting in his cruiser in the city's business district when he spotted an Orange VW Bug emerging from an alleyway behind a restaurant. Lee was curious as to what the vehicle was doing there since he knew that the restaurant closed at 10 p.m. on weeknights and it was now 1:30 in the morning. He decided to check it out and so he started up his vehicle, did a U-turn and pulled in behind the Bug, keeping his distance. While he did so, he radioed in the license tag and soon had a response – stolen. Lee then engaged his roof lights and signaled the driver of the VW to pull over.

Bundy had been in this situation before and he responded in exactly the same way. Rather than obey the officer's instruction, he floored the Bug and raced off in a vain attempt to outrun the police cruiser. That chase continued for about a mile before Bundy veered suddenly towards the side of the road and brought his car to a stop. But he wasn't about to concede defeat just yet. He obeyed when Lee ordered him from the vehicle and instructed him to lay face down on the tarmac. Then, as the officer tried to cuff him, he sprung suddenly into life.

Lee hadn't been expecting resistance and so he was caught by surprise when Bundy rolled over and kicked his legs out from under him. As Lee hit the deck, Bundy was on him, struggling desperately for the officer's revolver. Lee was younger and heavier than Bundy but Bundy fought with the desperation of a man with nothing to lose and his freedom to gain. During the scuffle a shot went off and that seemed to spur Bundy on. He wrenched himself free of Lee's grasp, jumped to his feet and set off down the middle of the road at a sprint. "Stop! Stop or I'll shoot!" Lee warned but Bundy wasn't listening. He was gaining ground, getting away. Then Lee raised the pistol, took aim and fired. In the road ahead, Bundy buckled and hit the deck and then lay still.

Officer Lee approached the prone figure cautiously. He wasn't sure whether he'd hit the suspect, let alone killed or seriously injured him. The man might have a gun, might be feigning injury, ready to shoot as Lee got closer. The officer approached, dropped to a knee and reached out a hand to check for a pulse. That was when Bundy burst into action again, knocking Lee off balance and grabbing his gun hand.

The fight this time was even more vicious. But eventually, the younger, stronger man prevailed. Eventually, he had Bundy pinned to the ground, his face pushed to the blacktop. As Lee fixed the cuffs into place he had no idea that the man he'd just captured was a notorious escaped killer, who currently occupied a spot on the FBI's Most Wanted List. "I wish you'd killed me," Bundy told the officer as he was being driven back into Pensacola.

Bundy was taken to a police station where he gave his name as 'Ken Misner' and his address as 509 College Avenue, Tallahassee. By the following morning, however, the word was out. Pensacola PD had captured America's most wanted serial killer. And it did not take long for the cops in Tallahassee and in Lake City to link him to the Chi Omega murders and the disappearance of Kimberley Leach. They had eyewitnesses to the Leach abduction, all of who picked out Bundy as the man driving the white van. They also had Leslie and Danny Parmenter, who had encountered Bundy in the K-Mart parking lot in Jacksonville.

And then there was the Chevy van that Bundy had been using. He'd been careful, as he always was, to wipe it clean of prints. But the vehicle delivered up other evidence – fibers that could be matched to Bundy's clothes; hairs similar to Kimberly's and blood that matched her type. As for the Chi Omega murders, the most compelling evidence was the bite marks left on Lisa Levy's buttocks. A cast was taken of Bundy's teeth and then sent to forensic odonatologist, Dr. Richard Souviron, for comparison. Souviron's response was that it was highly unlikely that anyone other than Ted Bundy could have inflicted the bites.

On April 7, came the news that investigators had long expected and that Kimberley Leach's parents had long feared. Kimberley's body was found in an abandoned pig shed in Suwanee State Park in Columbia County. The three months that the corpse had lain undiscovered had been hot and dry and the body was mummified rather than decomposed. Cause of death was difficult to determine although strangulation and bludgeoning (Bundy's usual methods of murder) were ruled out since there were no broken bones. The was, however, a definite incision to the neck area, leading the medical examiner to surmise that Kimberley Leach had been stabbed. There was also evidence of sexual assault, although again, the condition of the corpse made a more precise diagnosis difficult. What is certain, however, was that Kimberley Leach, the little girl who had so looked forwarded to her upcoming Valentine's Ball, had died in considerable terror and pain.

There was also further evidence linking Bundy to the crime. Semen on Kimberley's undergarments was matched to Bundy's type; cigarette butts found at the scene were of the brand that Bundy smoked – Winston's; dirt and leaves found on the tires and wheels of the impounded Chevy matched soil and vegetation at the crime scene; credit card receipts put Bundy in the area on the day of the abduction. It all added up to a compelling case with forensics, circumstantial evidence and eyewitness identification.

Bundy was charged with the murder of Kimberley Leach on July 31, 1978 and with the Chi Omega murders shortly after. He'd chosen a bad jurisdiction in which to commit capital homicide.

With the exception of Texas, the State of Florida executes more killers than any other.

Chapter 15: The Trials of Ted Bundy

Theodore Robert Bundy would face two separate murder trials, one four the Kimberley Leach murder, the other for the atrocities committed at the Chi Omega sorority house. The first of those (Chi Omega) came before the courts on June 25, 1979, in Miami, Florida and attracted media interest from across the country and indeed from around the world. The word was out by now. Horrendous as the Chi Omega murders were, they were only the tip of a very large iceberg. Ted Bundy was a monster in human form, suspected of brutally murdering as many as 36 young women. And although Bundy steadfastly denied killing anyone, he seemed to enjoy teasing and tantalizing his inquisitors. On one occasion a law officer asked him whether he'd really murdered 36 women to which Bundy responded that the officer should add one more digit to that number.

Bundy also sparked controversy during the trial by constantly firing and then re-instating his court-appointed lawyers. The first year law school dropout insisted that he could do a better job and appointed himself lead counsel, a bad move as it turned out. Bundy made major mistakes, including his decision to reject a pre-trial deal that would have spared him from the electric chair. During the trial itself, he horrified the jury (and most of the packed gallery) by pressing one of the police officers for graphic details of the Chi Omega crime scene. Bundy was quite obviously relishing the retelling of his horrific deeds. The only people in the courtroom who seemed unaffected were the 'Bundy groupies,' young women who took their places in the front row of the public benches every day to gaze adoringly at the handsome psychopath.

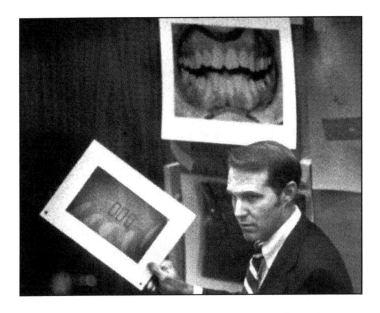

Dr. Richard Sauviron presenting dental evidence

In the end, though, there were two pieces of evidence that sunk Bundy. First there was the testimony of Nita Neary, the Co-Ed who had spotted the intruder in the Chi Omega house on the night of the murders. Neary had only seen the man in profile and he'd had a watch cap pulled over his eyes. But she was adamant it was Bundy and stuck to her identification under fierce cross-examination.

Even more damaging was the expert testimony given by Dr. Richard Souviron who reiterated his opinion that only Ted Bundy's teeth could have inflicted the wounds found on Lisa Levy. As Dr. Souviron described those bite marks, full-sized photographs of the bites were displayed on a screen and the doctor pointed out what made them unique when compared to Bundy's teeth. It was powerful stuff and must have weighed heavily on the decision that was ultimately made by the jury. On July 23rd, they deliberated for almost seven hours before returning to the courtroom with the verdict everyone had expected – guilty.

One week later, on July 30, Bundy was back in court for the penalty phase of the trial. The same jury that had condemned Bundy to death would determine his fate but only after they heard arguments for and against delivering the ultimate sentence.

One of those who spoke on Bundy's behalf was his mother, Louise, who made a stirring plea for mercy. She had never stopped believing in her son's innocence.

Bundy also took the stand to vehemently declare his innocence, blaming the media for pre-judging the case and thus poisoning the jury. "It is absurd to ask for mercy for something I did not do," he told the hushed courtroom, delivering his plea with such passion that there were undoubtedly those in the room who believed him. But the people who really counted in these proceedings were not swayed. The jury recommended electrocution and Judge Cowart, who had presided over both trials, affirmed that recommendation. Ted Bundy was going to the electric chair.

There was still, of course, the matter of the Kimberly Leach trial, even though the State of Florida was criticized for wasting public funds by pursuing charges when the defendant had already been condemned to death. It is not difficult to figure out why the State had decided to press ahead. Bundy was already filing appeals in the Chi Omega case. Should he succeed in having that verdict overturned, prosecutors wanted to have something to fall back on.

Bundy reacts angrily in court

Six months after the Chi Omega verdict, the Leach trial got underway on January 7, 1980. As in the previous trial, Bundy's team had applied for, and obtained, a change of venue, this time to Orlando, Florida. The trial would take place at the Orange County Courthouse. Mindful, perhaps, of the missteps during the earlier trial, Bundy decided to stand down this time and leave his defense in the hands of his public defenders. They suggested that he plead "not guilty by reason of insanity" and that approach made sense. It might be easy for a jury to believe that a man who committed such horrific acts was insane and an acquittal on those grounds would help his appeals in the Chi Omega case. But Bundy refused. Author Ann Rule, a close friend of Bundy's, stated in her book "The Stranger Beside Me," that the Ted she knew would rather be electrocuted than declared insane.

In terms of evidence, the Leach case was stronger than the Chi Omega case. Assistant State Attorney Bob Dekle presented sixty-five witnesses, all of who could link Bundy to the crime in one way or another, including the man who had seen Kimberly inside the white Chevrolet van. Then there was the forensic evidence lifted from the crime scene, from the victim's body, from the van itself. Taken together this evidence was fatal to the meager defense Bundy's team was able to muster. On February 7, the jury returned a verdict of guilty.

The penalty phase of Bundy's second trial got underway on February 9, 1980, which was coincidentally the second anniversary of Kimberly Leach's death. Bundy, however, had other things on his mind. Carol Ann Boone was one of his longtime supporters and their friendship had blossomed into a romance. Bundy had expressed his desire to marry Carol Ann but the warden of the prison had refused, saying that there would be no wedding "under his roof." Now, during the trial's mitigation phase, Bundy called Carol Ann to the stand and began questioning her about their relationship. Then the pair caught everyone off guard by exchanging vows. Since this had taken place under oath and in the presence of a judge, the agreement was official. The couple was legally married. Shortly after those vows were exchanged, the groom was sentenced to death by electrocution. He was transported to Raiford Penitentiary just outside of Starke, Florida to await his date with the executioner.

Chapter 16: Burn in Hell

Carrying out a judicial execution in the United States is a prolonged and expensive process with the condemned man entitled to countless appeals. Some prisoners spend years, even decades, on death row and Ted Bundy was certainly not going to go easily. Over the next nine years, he filed countless motions and appeals and in this he was actually helped by having been convicted in two separate trials. As soon as an execution date approached, he would file an appeal in the other conviction thus delaying the process. He had very little success via the court's though, with appeals to the Florida Supreme Court turned down in both the Chi Omega and Leach cases. During this time, Bundy attained a measure of celebrity and gave several high profile interviews including to Michaud and Aynesworth when he all but admitted to serial murder using the clever third party method.

Bundy also agreed to speak to Special Agent William Hagmaier of the FBI's Behavioral Science Unit. It was to Hagmaier that Bundy would explain the deep, underlying motive behind his murders. He said that murder was not about lust or violence but about possession. "The victim becomes a part of you," he said, "and you two are forever one. The grounds where you kill them or leave them become sacred to you, and you will always be drawn back to them."

Bundy also told Hagmaier that he had considered himself an "amateur," and an "impulsive killer" during his early years, before moving into what he termed his "prime" or "predator" phase with the murder of Lynda Healy. That implied that he had begun killing well before 1974 and sent investigators scrambling to identify unsolved homicides that might have been committed by Bundy. (Some of those cases are mentioned later in this book.)

Bundy being interviewed by William Hagmaier

Another man who interviewed Bundy was Dr. Robert Keppel who had been one of the investigators in the Washington Co-Ed murders. By the mid-80's, Keppel was hunting another psycho, 'The Green River Killer' and Bundy got in touch offering his help. His subsequent interviews with Keppel provided some fascinating insights into the mind of a serial sex slayer but got Keppel no closer to catching his killer. (Gary Leon Ridgeway would eventually be tried and convicted of the Green River murders.)

For Bundy, meanwhile, time was running out. When his final appeal was turned down by the US Supreme Court on January 17,

1989, he was all out of options. Florida Governor Bob Martinez immediately signed the death warrant, setting the date of Bundy's execution for January 24.

But still, Bundy's lawyers tried to buy him a bit more time, offering confessions and the locations of undiscovered bodies in an attempt to delay the inevitable. They even approached families of the victims and asked them to petition the Florida governor. All of those requests were refused but Bundy decided to confess anyway, granting time to investigators from Washington, Utah and Colorado. The man he chose to hear his confession to the Washington murders was his old nemesis, Bob Keppel.

Keppel was a man who had been around homicide investigations for most of his career and had hunted down some of America's most disturbed killers. But even he was shocked by what Bundy had to say. Bundy confessed that he was essentially a necrophile who was more interested in the corpses of his victims than in their living bodies. It was a compulsion that led him back to his dumping grounds again and again to engage in sexual acts with the decomposing corpses. While living in Utah, he'd once made a 600 mile round trip to Colorado to defile a victim's rotting corpse. He also admitted to decapitating some of his victims with a hacksaw and carrying their heads home with him. So extreme were some of Bundy's admissions that Keppel decided they should not be made public. All he would say was that they involved "compulsive necrophilia and extreme perversion."

As to the number of victims, Bundy was cagey, even in the shadow of the electric chair. He admitted to some murders and denied others. Yes, he'd murdered Donna Manson, Janice Ott and Denise Naslund. Yes, he'd killed Georgann Hawkins. He even named victims that the investigators were unaware of, two women in Idaho, for example. But he emphatically denied killing Ann Marie Burr, the young girl who had disappeared from his neighborhood when he was 14 years old. And he also denied that he was involved in the murder of Katherine Devine, a 14-year-old hitchhiker who was killed at around the time the 'Ted' murders started. In the end, he confessed to 39 murders, three more than the generally accepted number. Bob Keppel thinks it's more. He thinks that Bundy would have admitted to more murders if he'd had more time. Keppel thinks that as many as 100 women and young girls may have met their fate at Ted Bundy's hands. Whatever the truth, Bundy would take it with him to the grave.

Ted Bundy finally kept his date with Florida's 'Ol' Sparky' on Tuesday, January 24, 1989. He was a broken man by then, exhausted by nights without sleep, numbed by the sedatives he'd been given to still his panic. Many of those who had believed in his innocence were shocked by his eleventh-hour confessions. His mother was reportedly devastated by the admissions. So too was his wife, Carol Ann Boone. Carol, however, had long since jumped the Bundy ship and fled back to Seattle, taking Bundy's daughter, conceived during an illicit liaison during a prison visit, with her.

Commemorative t-shirts for sale before Bundy's execution

As the clocks inside the prison walls computed the last hours of Ted Bundy's life a huge crowd gathered outside. Parents even brought their children along. A carnival atmosphere endured with revelers singing, dancing and drinking beer. Many of them carried placards. "Burn Bundy!" one of them read, "It's Fry-day!" declared another.

At exactly 7 a.m. the door to the death cell swung open and Prison Superintendent Tom Barton stepped in, escorted by two guards. Bundy was then told to stand and his hands were cuffed. Then he was led to the execution chamber a short distance away, where he was strapped into the electric chair and the electrodes were attached to the shaven spots on his leg and head. He stared blankly through the Plexiglas partition at the twelve witnesses to the execution and then turned to his spiritual advisor, Reverend Fred

Lawrence. "Fred," he said. "I'd like you to give my love to my family and friends."

Warden Barton had one more call to make before the execution could proceed. He dialed the governor's number and was told that there would be no reprieve. Barton then hung up the phone and nodded to the hooded executioner who depressed the lever, sending a jolt of electricity through Bundy's body. Then the action was repeated. At 7:16, Bundy was declared dead, sparking wild scenes of celebration and a fireworks display outside the prison. A short while later, a white hearse emerged from the prison gates carrying the remains of America's most notorious serial killer.

Ted Bundy's body was later cremated. In accordance with his final request, his ashes were scattered over the Cascade Mountains, the place where he'd taken so many of his victims.

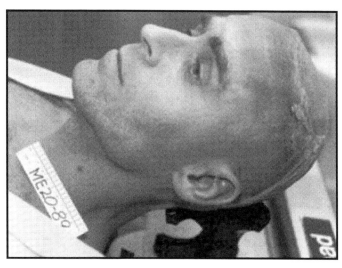

Bundy's body is removed from the execution chamber

Timeline

November 24, 1946: Born Theodore Robert Cowell in a home for unwed mothers in Burlington, Vermont.

October 1950: Bundy's mother, Louise, moves with her son to Tacoma, Washington.

May 19, 1951: Louise Cowell marries Johnny Bundy and her son takes his step-father's last name.

Spring 1965: Graduates from Woodrow Wilson High School in Tacoma, Washington.

Fall 1965: Enrolls at the University of Puget Sound. Attends the school until the Spring of 1966.

Fall 1966 to Spring 1969: Attends the University of Washington.

1967 to 1968: Involved in a relationship with Stephanie Brooks.

Fall 1968: Brooks ends the relationship.

Early 1969: Visits Burlington, Vermont, and learns for certain that he is illegitimate.

Fall 1969: Re-enters University of Washington

Fall 1969: Meets Elizabeth Kloepfer, who will remain his girlfriend throughout most of the murders.

Spring 1973: Graduates from the University of Washington.

Summer 1973: Begins courting Stephanie Brooks again. They become engaged.

December 1973: Abruptly ends his engagement to Stephanie Brooks

January 5, 1974: Attacks Karen Sparks in her Seattle apartment. Sparks survives.

February 1, 1974: Abducts Lynda Ann Healy from her basement bedroom in Seattle.

March 12, 1974: Abducts Donna Manson from the campus of Evergreen State College.

April 17, 1974: Abducts Susan Rancourt from Central Washington University.

May 6, 1974: Abducts Kathy Parks from the campus at Oregon State.

June 1, 1974: Murders Brenda Ball in Burien, Washington.

June 11, 1974: Abducts Georgann Hawkins from an alley near her University of Washington sorority house.

July 14, 1974: Janice Ott and Denise Naslund abducted from Lake Sammamish.

Fall 1974: Enters the University of Utah Law School.

September 2, 1974: Rapes and murders a still-unidentified hitchhiker in Idaho.

September 7, 1974: Skeletal remains of Janice Ott, Denise Naslund, and Georgann Hawkins are found

October 2, 1974: Abducts and murders 16-year-old Nancy Wilcox of Holladay, Utah. Nancy's body has never been found.

October 18, 1974: Abducts Melissa Smith from Midvale, Utah.

October 27, 1974: Melissa Smith's body is found in Summit Park near Salt Lake City, Utah.

October 31, 1974: Abducts Laura Aimee from Lehi, Utah.

November 8, 1974: Carol DeRonch escapes a Bundy abduction attempt.

November 8, 1974: Debby Kent abducted from a school in Bountiful, Utah.

October 1974: Laurie Aimee's body is found.

January 12, 1975: Abducts Caryn Campbell from a hotel in Aspen, Colorado.

February 18, 1975: Caryn Campbell's body is found.

March 3, 1975: The skulls of Lynda Ann Healy, Brenda Ball, Roberta Parks, and Susan Rancourt are found near Taylor Mountain in Washington.

March 15, 1975: Abducts Julie Cunningham from Vail, Colorado.

April 6, 1975: Abducts Melanie Cooley from her school in Nederland, Colorado.

April 23, 1975: Melanie Cooley is found dead twenty miles from Nederland.

May 6, 1975: Abducts Lynette Culver from her school playground in Pocatello, Idaho.

June 28, 1975: Abducts Susan Curtis from the campus of Brigham Young University while she is attending a youth conference.

July 1, 1975: Abducts Shelley Kay Robertson from Golden, Colorado.

August 16, 1975: Arrested for possession of burglary tools during a traffic stop in Salt Lake City.

March 1, 1976: Found guilty of aggravated kidnapping in the DeRonch case.

June 30, 1976: Sentenced to 1-15 years in prison.

June 7, 1977: Escapes from Pitkin County Law Library in Colorado while preparing for trial in the Campbell murder.

June 13, 1977: Apprehended in Aspen, Colorado.

December 30, 1977: Escapes from Garfield County Jail in Colorado.

January 8, 1978: Arrives in Tallahassee, Florida.

January 14, 1978: Enters the Chi Omega sorority house and murders Lisa Levy and Margaret Bowman. Severely injures Kathy Kleiner and Karen Chandler.

January 14, 1978: Attacks Cheryl Thomas in her home, seriously injuring her.

February 9, 1978: Abducts Kimberly Leach from her school in Lake City, Florida.

February 15, 1978: Arrested while driving a stolen VW in Pensacola, Florida.

April 12, 1978: Kimberly Leach's body is found in Suwanee State Park in Florida.

July 27, 1978: Indicted for the murder of Kimberley Leach.

July 31, 1978: Indicted for the Chi Omega murders.

July 07, 1979: Chi Omega murder trial begins.

July 23, 1979: Found guilty of the murders of Lisa Levy and Margaret Bowman.

July 31, 1979: Sentenced to death for the Levy and Bowman murders.

January 7, 1980: Kimberley Leach murder trial begins.

February 6, 1980: Found guilty of murdering Kimberly Leach.

February 9, 1980: Sentenced to death for Leach murder.

July 2, 1986: Obtains a stay of execution only fifteen minutes before he is scheduled to die.

November 18, 1986: Obtains a stay seven hours before his scheduled execution.

January 17, 1989: Final death warrant is issued.

January 24, 1989: Executed in the electric chair at Raiford Penitentiary, Florida.

Victims

Washington / Oregon

February 1, 1974: Lynda Ann Healy (age, 21): Bludgeoned while she slept and abducted. Skull later found on Taylor Mountain site.

March 12, 1974: Donna Gail Manson (19): Abducted while walking to a concert on the Evergreen State College campus. Body never found.

April 17, 1974: Susan Elaine Rancourt (18): Disappeared from Central Washington University. Skull recovered at Taylor Mountain site.

May 6, 1974: Roberta Kathleen Parks (22): Vanished from Oregon State University in Corvallis. Skull found at Taylor Mountain site.

June 1, 1974: Brenda Carol Ball (22): Disappeared after leaving the Flame Tavern in Burien, Washington. Skull recovered at Taylor Mountain site.

June 11, 1974: Georgann Hawkins (18): Abducted from an alley behind her sorority house. Skeletal remains recovered at Issaquah.

July 14, 1974: Janice Ann Ott (23): Abducted from Lake Sammamish. Skeletal remains recovered at Issaquah site.

July 14, 1974: Denise Marie Naslund (19): Abducted from Lake Sammamish within four hours of Janice Ott. Skeletal remains recovered at Issaquah site.

Utah / Colorado / Idaho

October 2, 1974: Nancy Wilcox (16): Murdered in Holladay, Utah. Bundy claimed to have buried her body but it was never found.

October 18, 1974: Melissa Anne Smith (17): Vanished from Midvale, Utah. Body found in mountains near the town.

October 31, 1974: Laura Ann Aime (17): Disappeared from Lehi, Utah. Body discovered in American Fork Canyon.

November 8: Debra Jean Kent (17): Vanished after leaving a school play in Bountiful, Utah. Body never found.

January 12, 1975: Caryn Eileen Campbell (23): Disappeared from the Willowild Inn in Aspen, Colorado. Body found on a dirt road close to the hotel.

March 15, 1975: Julie Cunningham: Disappeared from Vail, Colorado. Bundy claimed to have buried her body but it was never found.

April 6, 1975: Denise Lynn Oliverson (25): Abducted while bicycling to her parents' house in Grand Junction, Colorado. Body never found.

April 15, 1975: Melanie Cooley (18): Disappeared after leaving Nederland High School. Her bludgeoned and strangled corpse was discovered two weeks later in Coal Creek Canyon.

May 6, 1975: Lynette Dawn Culver (12): Abducted from Alameda Junior High School in Pocatello, Idaho. Bundy claims to have thrown her body into the Snake River, but it was never found.

June 28, 1975: Susan Curtis (15): Disappeared during a youth conference at Brigham Young University. Body never found.

Florida

January 15, 1978: Margaret Elizabeth Bowman (21): Bludgeoned and then strangled as she slept, Chi Omega sorority, Florida State University.

January 15, 1978: Lisa Levy (20): Bludgeoned, strangled and sexually assaulted as she slept, Chi Omega sorority, Florida State University.

February 9, 1978: Kimberly Diane Leach (12): Abducted from her junior high school in Lake City, Florida. Remains found in Suwannee River State Park.

Victims who Survived

January 4, 1974: Karen Sparks (18): Bludgeoned and sexually assaulted as she slept in her Seattle, Washington apartment.

November 8, 1974: Carol DaRonch (18): Attempted abduction in Murray, Utah. Escaped from Bundy's car.

January 15, 1978: Karen Chandler (21): Bludgeoned as she slept at Chi Omega sorority, Florida State University.

January 15, 1978: Kathy Kleiner (21): Bludgeoned as she slept, Chi Omega sorority, Florida State University.

January 15, 1978: Cheryl Thomas (21): Bludgeoned as she slept in her Tallahassee apartment within hours of the Chi Omega attacks.

Other possible victims

Bundy remains a suspect in a number of unsolved homicides, and is likely responsible for others that have not been identified. He once hinted to FBI Special Agent William Hagmaier that he started killing well before 1974. He also told Washington homicide investigator Robert Keppel that there were some murders he would never talk about because they were "too close to home" or involved victims who were "very young."

The following murders have been linked in one way or another to Ted Bundy.

Ann Marie Burr (age 8): Vanished from her home in Tacoma, Washington on August 31, 1961. The Burr home was on 14-year-old Ted Bundy's newspaper delivery route although he later denied any involvement in her disappearance. Ann Marie has never been found.

Lisa Wick and Lonnie Trumbull (both 20): Bludgeoned as they slept in their basement apartment in Seattle's Queen Anne Hill district on June 23, 1966. Trumbull died. Lisa Wick survived but with severe injuries and permanent memory loss.

Susan Davis and Elizabeth Perry (both 19): Stabbed to death near Atlantic City, New Jersey on May 30, 1969. Bundy was 60 miles away in Philadelphia during that timeframe. He later hinted to investigators that he'd killed two women in Atlantic City in 1969, while visiting family in Philadelphia. Family members reported that Bundy had been wearing an arm cast that weekend and claimed to have been injured in an auto accident. There is no evidence that such an accident occurred.

Rita Curran (24): Strangled, bludgeoned and raped in her basement apartment in Burlington, Vermont on July 19, 1971. There are suggestions that Bundy was back in his place of birth during the week and the crime scene had some similarities to those in Seattle.

Joyce LePage (21): Disappeared from Washington State University campus on July 22, 1971. Her skeletal remains were found nine months later, in a ravine south of Pullman, Washington.

Rita Lorraine Jolly (17): Disappeared from West Linn, Oregon on June 29, 1973. Her body has never been found.

Vicki Lynn Hollar (24): Went missing from Eugene, Oregon on August 20, 1973. Body never found. (Bundy later confessed to two murders in Oregon without naming the victims. Oregon detectives believe he was talking about Jolly and Hollar.)

Katherine Merry Devine (14): Disappeared while hitchhiking on November 25, 1973. Her body was found in Capitol State Forest near Olympia, Washington a month later.

Brenda Joy Baker (14): Last seen hitchhiking near Puyallup, Washington on May 27, 1974. Her body was found in Millersylvania State Park a month later.

Sandra Jean Weaver (19): Last seen alive in Salt Lake City, Utah on July 1, 1974. Her body was discovered near Grand Junction, Colorado a day later. Some sources suggest that Bundy mentioned her in his death row confessions.

Carol L. Valenzuela (20) Last seen hitchhiking near Vancouver, Washington on August 2, 1974. Her remains were discovered two months later in a shallow grave south of Olympia, along with those of another female later identified as Martha Morrison (17). Both women resembled typical Bundy victims, with long hair parted in the middle. Bundy drove the route from Seattle to Salt Lake City in early August 1974.

Nancy Perry Baird (23): Disappeared from the service station where she worked in Farmington, Utah on July 4, 1975. Body never found. Bundy denied involvement in this case during his death row interviews.

Debbie Smith (17): Disappeared from Salt Lake City during February 1976, shortly before Bundy went on trial for the DaRonch kidnapping. Her body was found near Salt Lake City International Airport on April 1, 1976.

Bibliography

Jeffries, H. Paul. *Profiles in Evil*. Warner Books (1992)

Kendall, Elizabeth. *The Phantom Prince: My Life with Ted Bundy*. Madonna Publishers (1981)

Keppel, Robert D., PhD. (with William J. Birnes). *Signature Killers*. Pocket Books (1997)

Keppel, Robert D., PhD. *The Riverman: Ted Bundy and I Hunt for the Green River Killer*. Pocket Books (1995)

Larsen, Richard W. *The Deliberate Stranger*. Prentice Hall (1980)

Michaud, Stephen & Aynesworth, Hugh. *The Only Living Witness: The Story of Serial Killer Ted Bundy*. Penguin Books (1989)

Michaud, Stephen & Aynesworth, Hugh. *Ted Bundy: Conversations with a Killer*. New American Library (1989)

Rule, Ann. *The Stranger Beside Me*. Norton (1996)

Schechter, Harold. *The Serial Killer Files*. Random House (2003)

Wilson, Colin & Wilson, Damon. *Written in Blood: A History of Forensic Detection*. Robinson (2003)

Wilson, Colin & Seaman Donald. *The Serial Killers: A Study in the Psychology of Violence*. Virgin Publishing Ltd (1992)

Winn, Stephen & Merrill, David. *Ted Bundy: The Killer Next Door*. Bantam (1980)

For more True Crime books by Robert Keller please visit

http://bit.ly/kellerbooks

40915753R00087

Printed in Poland
by Amazon Fulfillment
Poland Sp. z o.o., Wrocław